D0427660

Guided Imagery
Volume One

Larry Moen

UNITED STATES
P U B L I S H I N G

Published by: United States Publishing
                         3485 Mercantile Avenue
                         Naples, Florida 33942

Cover Art: Charles Frizzell ©
                         "All My Relations"

Printed in the United States of America.

Library of Congress Cataloging-in-Publication Data

Guided Imagery / [edited by] Larry Moen. — 1st ed.
        p.   cm.
    ISBN 1-880698-01-3 (v. 1) : $11.95
    1. Meditation. 2. Imagery (Psychology) 3. Visualization.
    4. Self-actualization (Psychology) I. Moen, Larry, 1948-.
    BF637.M4G85 1992
    153.3'2—dc20   91-45428
                                                        CIP

To my sons Matthew and Lucas.

Contents

Healing

Inner Guides/Teachers

Receiving Gifts and Love

Training and Control

Freedom and Awareness

Inner Child/Family

Creativity and Inspiration

Grief

Past Lives

Male/Female

Introduction

This first volume of GUIDED IMAGERY is a labor of love from the many contributors who are sharing their journeys with you. Although there are many wonderful books out on "how to" visualize, this is a unique compilation of guided journeys to help you deal with anxieties, relationships, stress, and to learn how to tap into your higher self. Our goals are simple — for you to be able to feel better and improve the quality of your life which, in turn, will improve the lives of all who surround you.

I was first introduced to guided imagery at a workshop entitled "Healing Your Inner Child" by Margot Escott. My journey in healing and opening up to the love that is available to all of us inspired me to pursue many paths of personal growth such as meditation, visualization, self-hypnosis, and Tai-Chi. While exploring these avenues I found that I was growing into a more calm, serene person. I also discovered that everyone has an inner core consisting of pure beauty.

I have been fortunate to have encountered many

wonderful people who have their own unique images. Some of these people are "professional" healers. But, for the most part, the guides who have contributed to this collection of guided imagery are individuals who have found ways that have helped themselves, and the people they love, attain inner peace.

Creative imagery and visualization have numerous benefits. It is now common knowledge that visualization is effective in treating stress related and physical illnesses including headaches, muscle spasms, chronic pain, etc. Many researchers have found that imagery is an important part of treatment programs for a variety of diseases. It has also been shown to improve memory.

Images have not only the power to heal but to take you to higher realms of knowledge and experiences. It is through practicing visualizations that many athletes achieve peak performance in their particular sports. Professional golfers and tennis players are among those who use these techniques to improve their games. Visualizing that you can successfully manage a situation will help you to confront and master that situation. Visualize yourself already accomplishing a goal and your mind and body will assume you have. You are what you think you are. If you think sad thoughts, you feel unhappy. If you think fearful thoughts, you feel anxious.

The key to using imagery successfully is to use it when you are deeply relaxed. Relaxation alone is a valuable tool to have in your life. When you are relaxed you will be able to experience the images more vividly, so they are likely to have a more profound effect. The deeper your state of meditation or relaxation, the more vivid the detail. If you draw a blank or weak image say to yourself, "If I could see an image what would it be?" The images will become more real with practice. Give yourself time. Remember that these are merely techniques to help you use the imagination that you already have and use in many ways in your everyday life.

For example, think about your kitchen at home; just close your eyes and imagine what that room looks like. Next, see if you can remember all the colors in your kitchen. Then, imagine that you open the refrigerator door. Reach into the freezer, take out a piece of ice in your right hand. You may find that you experience a cool sensation even though you aren't actually touching a piece of ice. Now imagine taking a piece of lemon, slicing it, taking that slice and putting it into your mouth and taking a bite. Did you start to salivate? These are examples of guided imagery. You now see that you do have the ability to visualize.

As a potter molds his clay, you are capable of molding yourself into any direction you choose. You can change your programming.

At the conclusion of each journey you will find a quote from each guide, which you may wish to first read. These will give you some indication about the benefit or use of each particular journey.

You may wish to take turns reading the journeys with a friend, spouse, child or relative. If no one is available, then read your favorite journeys into a tape recorder and play them back at your leisure. It is said people are more receptive to suggestion when hearing their own voice. After the journey, you have several options: write, verbalize, draw, or meditate on the experience.

When reading some of the journeys, you will notice the word "pause" inserted in various places. The "pause" may last one second to one hour. The time allocated for each pause also may be determined beforehand.

You may also want to play some music, very spiritual or sensual. Since you are using all of your senses on the journeys, try to hear the music over the entire surface of your body. Remember, you are taking sensory voyages, creating scenes in your mind's eye, so vivid it will be as if you were actually there.

You will develop greater self-awareness and self-love and realize your full potential as a spiritual being having a human experience. You will communicate with your subconscious, your most valuable teacher.

We all have an inner guide that leads and protects us. It is my sincere hope that you will be able to make contact with yours, so that you can become the person you were truly meant to be.

May you obtain inner peace, love, serentiy and happiness for the good you accomplish by guiding yourself and others.

Good luck and happy images!

— *L. M.*
March 1992

Relaxation and Stress Release

1

Anger Release

Guide: Jule Scotti Post, M.S.

The Journey

Take this time for yourself — to heal, to release, to relax and attune yourself to your inner being. Begin by bringing your attention to the lower part of your body, from the waist down. Now as you count slowly from one to seven, tense all the muscles in your stomach, lower back, thighs, calves, feet and toes. Hold this tension. As you count down from seven to one, gradually release this tension so that all the muscles from your waist down to your toes become very deeply relaxed.

Pause

Now bring your attention to the upper part of your body, from your waist up. As you count from one up to seven, tense all the muscles in your chest, your back, your arms and hands, your shoulders, your neck, your head and face. Hold this tension. As you count down from seven to one, gradually release all this tension so that all the muscles from your waist up to your head become very deeply relaxed.

Pause

Now that your body is feeling deeply relaxed, picture yourself, in your mind's eye, in a situation that makes you feel very angry. See the situation clearly. Perhaps there are people involved. Notice where you are, and what you are saying or hearing said, if appropriate. Let yourself move fully into the time of this experience. Now be aware of how you feel this anger in your body. Perhaps it is a churning in your stomach, a tightness in your throat, or a strong pressure in your head. Sometimes when we are very angry we feel we want to cry.

Pause

When you have released your anger, you may feel ready to move towards forgiveness. If so, visualize the person(s) who elicits your angry feelings. Now see them completely surrounded by light. Repeat to yourself the phrase: "I forgive you and I forgive myself." Continue until you can say it from your heart. Feel the relief forgiveness brings to your inner being.

Pause

Now it is time to let go of anger. It is time to leave behind those feelings that were keeping you stuck, blocking your growth. Let yourself move to another time. To springtime in a beautiful flower garden, surrounded by blossoming cherry and apple trees. As you walk down the brick path between the flower beds, you see a collage of color, of all your favorite flowers. You look to see which ones are there. As you breathe in deeply, smell the air thick with the sweet gragrance of blossoms and flowers; listen to the birds singing. Now you come to a beautifully carved wood bench. Sit here quietly feeling the hard strength of the wood, the smooth texture of its surface. Take in the peacefulness of the garden. Let your mind rest on thoughts of the future that you would like to create for yourself when you are free of angry feelings that cloud your inner vision. You have the power to decide, to choose, to plan your own growth. Release your creative energy and enjoy whatever comes to you.

Pause

Gradually begin to bring yourself back now to your body, to the room around you, to the day, the time of the present moment. As you open your eyes remember the calling of your inner visions and go into your life with renewed strength, rooted in your inner being, growing up to the light.

"I like to remember that in the Chinese philosophy of the five elements, there is a direct, though not causal, relationship between the emotion of anger and the faculty of vision. Blocked anger may inhibit our inner vision. This imagery therefore works with both these aspects of the wood element."
— *Jule Scotti Post, M.S.*

2

Empty Jar

Guide: Liz Bachtel

The Journey

First, uncross everything... legs... arms... hands... loosen anything that feels tight or constraining... collars... belts... shoes... jewelry. Keeping your spine straight, your shoulders relaxed, your feet making contact with the earth, allow the chair to support your body. As we go within to focus on the breath, I invite you to allow your eyes to close...

Gently now, bring your awareness to your breathing... begin to relax now as you breathe in and out... in and out.... Notice the wonder of your breath... cool against the back of your throat as you breathe in... warm as you breathe out... observe... relax... breathe.

As you grow more relaxed, you breathe more deeply, more slowly. Allow your breath now to move to other parts of your body... to find and to dispel your tension.... Your neck and shoulders hold so much... breathe in and with your next breath... breathe out that tension... arms, hands and fingers that do so much... breathe in appreciation of what they do and breathe out that tension.... Move now to your chest.... Breathe in gratitude for your heart, your lungs... breathe out any tightness.... Move gently now to your belly... allow it to be soft... let your breath move up from your belly... breathe out deeply from this intuitive part of yourself.... Notice buttocks and allow this chair to support you.... You don't have to do a thing... breathe in rest and relaxation.... Notice legs, thighs, knees, calves, ankles... how well they have carried you today.... Breathe in "thank you...." Breathe out their tiredness. Be aware of your feet, toes... how strong and supportive they have been... allow earth now to support your feet that have so well supported you... breathe deeply and relax.

As you breathe now, allow your breath to move lightly over your entire body dispelling any remaining tension. You relax more and more deeply with every breath.

Very gently, now... move to your mind... your third eye.... Visualize, if you will... a clear glass jar. It is empty. Observe yourself now as you unscrew the lid and remove it. Look closely at this empty jar, become aware that it is waiting to be filled. Take now the burdens, the busyness of your day... your activities... your work... your many tasks... your errands... your travel... your apprehensions... your anxiety... your cares... your pain.... Observe now as one by one you place them into the jar. Continue now to fill the jar with any remaining bit of your day. Carefully and deliberately now, replace the lid on the jar. Give the lid one extra turn.

Breathe deeply now and observe that you stand and begin to carry the jar toward a door. Open the door. Outside, on the front step is a large shiny aluminum trash can. Open its lid now and place your jar inside.... Know that you may dispose of it now and forever... or return for it at another time, if you wish.... Put the lid back on the trash can... turn from it... walk back through the door. Lock the door and return to your chair.

Become aware once again of your breathing.... You are in the here and now... ready to be fully present... refreshed... relaxed... in body and in mind...

Breathe quietly now for a few more moments and as you feel ready... begin to make small gentle movements.... Let your body begin to stir... and when you are ready... open your eyes.

"This meditation is very effective when I need to begin a task which requires full attention and focus such as writing or studying. I've used this at the beginning of my night graduate classes and students find it very useful in order to "fully arrive" at class."
— Liz Bachtel

3

Free Fall

Guide: Angela Passidomo Trafford

The Journey

Feel your body relaxing. Feel your mind beginning to slow down. Every breath you take brings you deeper inside yourself, to a source of unconditional love and peace. Every breath you take makes you feel more relaxed... more at peace within yourself. It feels so wonderful just to lay back and to relax.

As you relax, visualize your thoughts as a flock of gentle lambs, and you are standing among the lambs with a magic wand. In your hands this magic wand has the power to cause each of the little lambs to lay down to rest in the green pasture. You walk among the lambs touching each lamb in turn with your magic wand. Each lamb gazes up at you with gentle, soulful eyes and lays down to rest in the green pasture. One by one you subdue the beautiful little lambs with your magic wand until you alone are standing in command. You alone are in charge and all the little lambs are at rest at your feet in the green pasture. Your mind is completely at peace. In this feeling of peace there is freedom.

8

Allow yourself to experience a sense of inner peace and freedom as your body deeply relaxes.

Visualize within your heart a beautiful inner flame. Your heart is made out of a hard, red wax. As you breathe, your breath fans this inner flame of unconditional love and passion for life. You can feel your heart softening as this beautiful flame grows brighter and brighter. Your heart softens as this beautiful feeling of warmth and heat and energy melts your heart, and you can feel your heart opening, and all the unconditional love and peace pouring forth from your heart and flowing into all of your internal organs, giving you a message of unconditional love and peace. And this unconditional love and peace is *who you are.* You feel the warmth of this beautiful radiation of love flowing through your inner self and warming any frozen spaces within yourself. You feel these feelings coming alive again as the love for yourself warms your being and melts all of your fears and reserves. You feel this warmth and energy warming you as you deeply, deeply relax. As you relax you feel this beautiful unconditional love. You feel it as a beautiful white light and within this beautiful white light of joy and peace is your authentic self. This white light is *who you are.* Relax into the experience of being who you are. This white light of unconditional love and peace, joy and acceptance is untouched by any of the pain of your life. You relax into this beautiful feeling of unconditional love and peace. Relax into being who you are.

Pause

As you relax further, visualize within yourself the rushing waters of a beautiful waterfall in a tropical paradise. This waterfall is tumbling down upon the beautiful cliffs within yourself. You see the green of the vegetation, the lush ferns. You visualize the waterfall as a beautiful, emerald green. You find yourself longing to climb to the top of this beautiful, cascading waterfall. You feel the rich earth beneath your feet as you climb to the very top and take in the beautiful magic of this paradise and its lush green vegetation. You feel inner peace and serenity. As the birds wheel in the sky overhead, you feel yourself letting go and falling — falling — falling in freedom. As you let yourself go, you visualize the cool, green pool beneath you. You free fall in to an acceptance of who you are. Just as you near the bottom of the waterfall, you feel a tropical breeze lift you up in the air. It lifts you higher and higher; you feel the support of the universe and the support of God in this lush tropical breeze. It lifts you higher and higher to the outer reaches of the universe.

Pause

From this place, you look down at yourself, at your life on earth, and you feel your life from a new perspective. Feel the serenity and the detachment of this point of view. Feel how much freedom it allows you. As you do, feel yourself beginning to merge within yourself. The light within allows you to merge into a beautiful totality of being and to experience the wholeness and wonder of being who you are. You experience a harmony of your body, mind and heart. Your body, mind and spirit are in perfect wholeness and order for healing and health. Allow yourself to rest in the love of the experience of being who you are. Feel yourself touching base within yourself, with your feeling self. Feel the freedom of this experience. Now bless yourself for taking this time for you.

Pause

Allow yourself again, to begin to surface back into consciousness. Know that you are honored, that you are worthy, and that you are loved. When you feel comfortable and ready, open your eyes.

"Relaxing the mind with tender, loving imagery allows us to touch base with our feeling self. The inner flame of unconditional love warms the heart, and opens us to receive gifts of grace and healing. As we let go of fear and free fall into acceptance, trust and love, we experience the divine support of God and are released into the flow of life in safety, protection and joy.

— Angela Passidomo Trafford

4

Magic Carpet

Guide: Karen M. Thomson, Ph.D.

The Journey

Stretch out on the floor with your feet about two feet apart and your toes rolled away from each other. Place your hands about two feet from your body, palms up. From the base of your spine to the top of your head, you are in a straight line and are feeling very relaxed. This is a rest position which in Yoga is called The Sponge, or The Corpse, and in this position, you are completely relaxed.

Go into very slow, deep breathing. As you inhale, count... slowly... to the end of the inhalation. Hold the breath to half of the count you had on the inhalation. When you're ready to exhale, count to the same number of your inhalation. Before inhaling again, count to half of the inhalation. For example: Inhale one... two... three...four... five... six... Hold... one... two... three... Exhale... one... two... three...four... five... six... Hold... one... two... three. Keep the concentration on your breathing and breathe for as long as you like. Allow the floor to support you as you, with every breath that you take, enter into a deeper and deeper state of relaxation and also a greater sense of awareness of a very peaceful feeling that you are beginning to experience.

Pause

As the meditation continues and you enter into an altered state of consciousness, know that you can come out of it at any time simply by opening your eyes.

Feeling very peaceful and completely and totally relaxed, imagine filling and surrounding yourself with a beautiful white Light which will remain with you, protecting, guiding, blessing and healing you. Where there is Light, there can be no darkness. You are feeling so relaxed that you feel very, very light, as light as a feather, in fact, lighter than a feather. The feeling is more as if you were like a helium balloon, so light that you could gently float up toward the ceiling. Imagine yourself now on a Magic Carpet which is lifting you up, for you feel that you are gradually and gently moving up toward the ceiling, floating up. There is no fear, for you are completely protected in pure white Light in this very airy state of consciousness. You are so light that you now float through the ceiling and the roof, and up above the trees and into the sky. If you like, you can look back to where you've just come from and the roof and the tree tops are gradually getting smaller and appear as they would appear if you were in an airplane.

Pause

You stretch out on your Magic Carpet as you glide up, up, up and now move through a cloud. You emerge from the cloud and feel the warm sunshine on your face, and it now warms your entire body. Every cell in your body breathes in this warm, gold Light that balances, heals, and rejuvenates every cell in your body. You are so high up now that you look back toward Earth, and it appears as a beautiful ball of light. See Earth now surrounded in a beautiful rose pink Light.

Pause

When you're ready to come back, feel the Magic Carpet beginning to make a slow descent as it floats to and fro ever so gently back toward earth. There is a beautiful soft, billowy cloud which you gracefully and ever so quietly move down through. The tops of the trees are becoming visible as you look over the side of the Magic Carpet, which continues to descend slowly. As your roof comes into view, you feel an immense gratitude for the Magic Carpet ride. It has been a "time out" for you and you are returning relaxed, free, ready to meet your responsibilities and obligations. Feel yourself now peacefully coming down now through your roof and gently taking your place on the floor where you started your journey. Take a deep breath and be aware of your body and the fact that it has been energized, rejuvenated, rested and is ready to go now where you need to go. Take a deep breath, open your eyes, and continue to be at Peace!

"I use the 'Magic Carpet' meditation when I want to 'get away' without physically leaving my home and when I don't want to read or watch television. It is an imaginary trip which provides many of the same benefits of a mini-vacation."
— *Karen M. Thomson, Ph.D.*

5

Medicine Place

Guide: Janet Doucette

The Journey

Begin with mindful breathing. Sit straight with the spine erect, hands placed gently on your thighs. Settle in as you breathe in and allow the breath to spiral down, around and through you, nourishing your cells and organs, replenishing the blood and lymph system. Relax and release the toxins and the tension accumulated during the day. Release them with the exhaled breath, out into the white light, where they are absorbed. Sense your chakra energy centers opening one by one, spinning freely in a clockwise fashion.

You are walking down a hallway with many doors. Pause at each door and look it over carefully. Choose the door that beckons you. Notice its material, color, shape of door knob. Open the door and walk down the stairway. Ten, nine, eight steps. Seven, six, five, four steps. Three, two, one step more; now stepping onto a beautifully tiled parquet floor.

Pause

Take a deep breath and then release it. Be mindful of the breathing, staying in the present, watching, accepting what comes to you. There is a mist gathering about you and the quality of feeling is light, intelligent, joyful. You may take time now to change your clothing or your appearance. When you are ready, step out from the cloak of mist. See before you a high stone wall. There is an open gate in this stone wall through which only you can pass. It is the gateway to a magnificent and eternal place. Walk through the gateway now, stepping over the boundary between worlds. And now before you is a special place, a garden of your spirit where everything you plant grows and continually blooms or bears foliage. There is a bench in this garden. Please sit on this bench. It may be of stone, wrought iron or wood. Look at it carefully and run your fingers across it. Take note now of your surroundings, your plantings and their essential order or random wildness. Notice what you have planted and where. You may hear water falling from high rocks, or bubbling down a shallow stream. This magical place of peace and symmetry is of your creation. No one may change a thing here. And no one may enter against your wishes. Take care to be mindful of the breath. See yourself as a being in constant outer vibration and yet with inner stillness. Hear the sounds of birds, water, wind and tree branches whispering about you. Then focus on that strange silence within.

Pause

As you breathe in the healing white light of your medicine place and release the tensions or anxiety which may have surfaced, concentrate on that particular silence within. Grasp it with your intent, your curiosity, your respect. Like a tunnel of darkness surrounded by light, the silence beckons you. Deeper you go, touching walls inlaid with crystal, signifying your clear mind and single purpose. The silence is all around you, touching you like soft cotton balls, pushing on your aura, joining you. It is perfect peace. As you experience this silence, totally accept its stillness, its unvarying sense of peace and quietude. Above your head a falling star streaks across the heavens. It plummets to the earth and sends out a radiant beam of light that shimmers like a wave of heat and envelopes you in a conscious quality of feeling. Recognize this feeling, find words that express the quality of this sensation.

Pause

Come back to consciousness and realizie with a clear mind that you can return to this medicine place whenever you want. As you flex your wrists and stretch your legs, breathe deep and full. Spend time discussing the silence and the quality of feelings that you felt. Share the message of the beam of light.

"I use this meditation to establish my 'garden' and associate with it. This helps me to relax into another meditation."
— *Janet Doucette*

6

Nature

Guide: Doss Knighten, M.S.

The Journey

Position yourself comfortably in a chair or lying down. Begin by taking deep breaths, and as you breath deeply allow yourself to relax. Each time you exhale, you will feel a greater sense of relaxation.

As you imagine yourself moving into a very relaxed state, allow yourself to begin to imagine, in any manner you would like, whether it be visual, auditory, kinesthetic or in any other manner you find suitable. Direct yourself on a trip into nature, where you will drift and relax. You pass through the woods finding yourself in a very, very relaxed comfortable place. It might be a meadow or lake surrounded by trees. Overhead you see the blue sky with white fluffy clouds. You observe the birds drifting about. You can feel the cool breezes blowing on your skin and you find this very relaxing and peaceful. As you look about, you see the details of the trees and the rocks and the blades of grass. As you observe the details of this scene you find this to be very relaxing. You allow yourself to relax deeper and deeper. Allow yourself to experience being here in this image and feel yourself sitting on the ground with the warm sun shining down. You are freely drifting at peace, imagine yourself warm, comfortable and at peace.

Pause

Imagine a person entering the scene with you to be a part of the experience. Select anyone you wish; perhaps choose one of your close personal friends. One who you would enjoy being with you, and that you would enjoy sharing this experience with. You are relaxing deeper and deeper and the person with you is relaxing deeper and deeper as well. You are now stepping into a canoe with your friend. As the two of you move out into the lake, paddling and stroking slowly, you find yourselves moving effortlessly toward a greater sense of peace. This is an experience that you are able to share and enjoy — the sense of quiet, the sense of peace. The sense of communion with nature is about you. Imagine saying to your friend those thoughts and feelings that you would like to share.

Pause

As you continue the relaxation, you also continue the image of drifting across the lake. Stroking the paddle slowly, you feel the canoe gliding along quietly and effortlessly. As the scenery of the lake passes by, the sense of relaxation, peace and joy that you are now experiencing will remain with you for a long, long time. As you return to your normal state you will recall this image and find it to be peaceful, relaxing and easily recreated whenever you wish.

As you return to the normal state allow yourself to feel peaceful, relaxed and again in tune with yourself and with the nature about you.

7

Relaxation or Sleep

Guide: Madeleine Cooper, MSW

The Journey

Settle down comfortably in your chair; feet flat on the floor, or if you are using this as a sleep meditation, snuggle into your bed. Pull the covers up if you wish. Let yourself relax. When you are comfortable you will start your special breathing. Breathe in the energy through your nose and exhale through your mouth... in with the fresh air and energy. As you exhale all the tensions start to leave you... relax... in through your nose... exhale feeling the tension leave you... in... out... continue your special breathing.... Your face feels relaxed.... Your shoulders are relaxed.... The muscles of your back are relaxed.... You let all the tensions go.... Your whole body is relaxed.... Just let it happen. Now let your breathing return to its natural rhythm. You find each time you practice relaxation, it will come more and more quickly, more and more deeply as tension slips away. Let the relaxation take over.

To deepen this relaxation, imagine yourself on a mountain path. The air is clean and fresh. It is late afternoon in the summer. The pine trees stand tall and stately to your right. You hear the rustle of aspen to your left. Your eye catches the shimmering of the leaves in the soft breeze. The path slopes downward. It has been cleared — pine needles brushed to the side. You are sure-footed and secure as you walk the earthen path leading in the direction of a meadow ahead. As you reach the edge of the line of trees, you see a hammock between two pine trees. You get into the hammock easily and rock gently. One finger trails the ground making an arc of leaves and pine needles and miniature pebbles. The hammock has a rough texture, but it is comfortable and very safe.

You can see the meadow below you with its carpet of wild flowers spread out... blue, red, white, coral, splashes of green... sunlit... bees humming... a dragonfly flits by.

You look up through the canopy of trees and see a blue sky with high white clouds going by. It is serene, beautiful, peaceful.... You gently rock in the hammock inhaling the energy, the life force and exhaling all tensions... all concerns. The air, rustling leaves, the drifting clouds, the scent of pine, the rough texture of the hammock all bring a special calm... sense of peace... a sense of inner nourishment.

An owl flies by and lights on a branch above you. It doesn't frighten you. Rather you feel a sense of curiosity. You continue to lie there in your hammock looking at the owl. The owl is looking at you. It ruffles its feathers before settling comfortably.... Something passes between you... some unspoken communication.... You have a feeling of inner confidence. Your feeling of relaxation is deeper. Allow yourself the time to relax.

The owl flies away. You watch the clouds drifting in large white puffs pushing one another more rapidly than before.... It is misting.... The soft touch of moist air is on your cheeks. You stop rocking and touch the dampness on your face. You know it's going to rain. You can already hear the first drops falling on the leaves nearby. You leave your hammock and start walking up the mountain path.

If you are using this as a sleep meditation, you will continue to sleep, then wake up relaxed and refreshed at the time you choose. If this is not a sleep meditation you come back to your waking state knowing you can return to your special place whenever you wish. It is a place where you can stretch out on your hammock and watch the clouds drift by... a place where rest and peace and inner healing take place.

You go up the path and with five steps now, you are more and more wide awake and aware of your surroundings. One up the hill, two feeling better than ever before, coming awake, bringing a sense of relaxation and peace, three feeling refreshed — as though you have had a refreshing, invigorating nap, four energizing, five eyes open... alert... wide awake... stretch... smile.... Have a wonderful day.

"Self confidence in one's inner wisdom is symbolized by the owl. The professional use of this sequence helps the client with issues of self esteem and inner confidence. The meditation is used without the owl sequence to induce relaxation in preparation for other discussion or for sleep. I personally use it for a ten minute respite." — *Madeleine Cooper*

8

Rest Well

Guide: Geneva B. Mitchell, D.C.H.

The Journey

Close your eyes. See yourself as you desire to be. Just imagine a clear golden glowing light surrounding your body. Keep the light around you as we begin our journey together. We are going to stretch and be. So when you are ready let's begin.

It's a clear, beautiful July morning. You are on an island. The island is or anywhere you desire and anyone or no one is along. Look up into the sky; notice a few thin clouds and hear and finally locate seagulls drifting and swooping, their every movement is easy and slow. You move easy and slow. Then you may decide to not move and just be. You find a shady spot on a sloping hill that overlooks the ocean and lean back, close your eyes and drift, dream or sleep. Hear my voice, the seagulls or not. It's not important. All is well and wonders are all around you. And golden light surrounds all and you. Freedom feels free. You are freedom. So, with your eyes closed and feeling light or heavy, you dream beautiful dreams of interesting events and places. Dream of a house with grassy sloping lawns, wide porches around water, a stream in front of the house, children playing, laughter, fun, running games.

Pause

Enter the house, feel at home, find your place. Relax. Go into the deepest part of you and see sincerity, freedom, intelligence, pure joy and talent. See and feel a new level of communication with all those involved in your life. A new awareness of control over all and every part of your life, freedom from anxiety, stress, control. Allowing others the same freedom and control, drift, down, down, down, feel nothing, hear only selected phrases.

Pause

Feel only love, conscious of none or all of the above. On the way to all of your goals, dreams and desires, you are aware of all that is of importance. Free from useless baggage, emotions and feeling; powerless findings gone. Strong feelings get stronger, more powerful than ever before, knowing of abilities beyond imaginings or expectations. Breathe in positive power. Breathe it all in finally so-o-o-o good now — go deeper — sleep and rest — So-o-o good, let go and be.

Pause

The sea sings to you so you're there or here or anywhere and it's O.K. There is no time here so it's O.K to drift deeper and rest. All organs rest, heart rhythm good, blood flows good. Muscles, nerves, brain, spinal cord, and vertebrae in line. Now freedom, perfection go on into sleep. Set your time to awaken, it's o.k. You're being served by the master within this wonderful creation, you. Only you say when you return and you may choose soon. When you do, if you do, count to 3. Slowly or sleep. All is good, very good. All is fine. Very fine. Free.

"I use this after the initial session for a feeling of peace and comfort and power over self." — *Geneva B. Mitchell*

9

Sensory Soother

Guide: Edie Weinstein-Moser, M.S.W.

The Journey

Allow your self to begin by drawing in one... full... deep and easy breath. As the air flows into your body, imagine that it contains soothing properties. Each portion of your body that it touches, can only relax... then when you release the breath, the air that flows from your body carries the tension that you may have been feeling when you began. Let it go... see it moving from your body. When you bring in the next breath, feel it moving to an even deeper place within you, soothing and relaxing even more of your body and bringing up even more tension, even more toxins, releasing even more tightness... You may need to consciously think about each breath you take, but soon it will come very naturally.

Pause

Just for a moment, be aware of any place in your body that feels uncomfortable. Say the word to yourself, like "head" or "neck" or "foot." Then, as you take your next breath, send the air to those parts of your body, allowing them to relax. See in that vivid imagination of yours, your toes uncurling, knots untying or any stiffness being soothed, like wrinkles being ironed out of a shirt. Ah... That's it...Now that you are relaxing more and more deeply in your body, feel growing sense of ease moving into your mind, just like a fine mist... See the mist in any color that you find soothing. Continue to breath it in and watch it curl around your thoughts, gently embracing them and reminding them that this is your time to be at peace, to be at ease, regardless of whatever is happening in your life. All that is real is the here and now, so let it be....

Pause

If troubling thoughts arise, that's all right...Let them be and send the mist to surround them. Watch what happens when you do that... Good... Now that you are moving deeper and deeper into peace and ease, imagine that you are standing in a beautiful place. Because this is your time, you may choose any place that gives you the feeling of tranquility. It may be somewhere you have visited or somewhere you have always wanted to go... It's up to you. Drink in this place with all of your senses keenly attuned. See the colors... shapes... designs.

Pause

Hear the sounds of music... or voices... or laughter... perhaps there are birds or animals around you.

Pause

Draw in a breath and smell something delightful...the sense of smell evokes powerful memories for us, so choose a smell that reminds you of something pleasant and soothing.

Pause

Reach out and touch the objects or people or creatures

around you gently, curiously as if for the very first time.... Perhaps you feel a breeze caressing your skin... or ruffling your hair... or the sun gently glowing on your face.

Pause

Is there something to taste...maybe a cool refreshing tropical fruit flavored beverage... or a rich creamy piece of chocolate... Savor the flavor of what you find there.

Pause

Now that your senses are feeling fully alive, check in with your thoughts and feelings and bodily sensations. What is happening within you? Take a few more moments to immerse yourself in this experience.

Pause

Now take one last... long look around you, knowing that you may return anytime you choose. This is your place and will always belong to you... but for now, it is time to return to this room... this time... this place... Take another deep breath and ever so slowly, become aware of the sensation of what is supporting you, anything you are experiencing with those finely tuned senses of yours and when you are ready, gently open your eyes, moving and stretching as you need to... Welcome back.

"This technique is designed to assist in reducing stress, lowering blood pressure, reducing muscular tension and providing for a safe haven in which the individual may resolve problems. It is most effective when done in a dimly lit, quiet, comfortable room. It is to be used in tandem with soothing music. I recommend anything by Daniel Kobialka, Mark Kelso, George Winston or Steven Halpern. A prone position is suggested, although some people are comfortable sitting." — *Edie Weinstein-Moser, M.S.W.*

10

Smile®

Guide: Norton Wyner, Ph.D.

The Journey

As your breathing slows into relaxed regularity, your imagination awaits the start of this wonderful trip of change. The rhythm of your breathing merges into all of the regular rhythms of the universe. The rhythm of time and tides. The rhythm of our planet orbiting in space.

And around our planet is yet another rhythm — the steady certainty of our moon rising each night. Imagine for a moment now the full moon as our imaginings have often regarded it... yes, imagine the full moon with a smiling face. A smile that is centuries old. Perhaps older than man himself. A smile that tells us that no matter what, we shall persist and overcome. A ~~benevolent~~, radiant smile that comes back time after time.

Yes, sometimes clouds cover the smiling moon. Other times, storms and other adversities hide the smiling moon. Hidden or not, we know it's always there. And sooner or later it triumphs and returns to view, gladdening our hearts. A

28

reminder that no matter what assails us...no matter what adversity besets us...no matter what new event sets us back...we are one with the inevitable triumphant flow of the moon and the universe.

And though like the man-in-the-moon, you may be beset by storm-like adversity from time to time, know that the healthy, vibrant you may be hidden but nevertheless there. So now proceed to push away the clouds of your [behavior], to reveal, to renew, to reinvigorate that healthy, best of yourself...

"Our SMILE® program is used with stress patients suffering from Persistent Chronic Recidivism — they "roll" from one stress symptom to the next, chronically relapsing. This introductory guided imagery is designed to provide a logical metaphor for their recurring relapses, while reassuring them of the certainty of overcoming recidivism." — Norton Wyner, Ph.D.

11

Stress Management

Guide: Jule Scotti Post, M.S.

The Journey

Begin the process of relaxation by taking a few deep breaths. As you breathe out, let go of any tension in your body. Let it flow out of you with your breath. As you breathe in, take in that life giving, nourishing oxygen and see it now flowing all around your body, bringing new energy to each cell. As you breathe in take in calmness, take in peacefulness, take in deep relaxation. As you breathe out, you let go more and more. Let yourself sink down deeper and deeper into relaxation.

In your mind's eye, picture a small ball of radiant light resting on the top of your head. See that light flowing around the top of your head, and around the back of your head. Let any tension in the muscles in your head dissolve in that warm flowing light. Let all those muscles become very deeply relaxed. See that light flowing around your face, across your forehead, around your eyes, your cheeks and down under your chin. Let any tension in the muscles of your face dissolve in that warm flowing light. Let all those muscles becomevery deeply relaxed. See that light now flowing down around your neck, around the back of your neck,and around the front of your neck. Let any tension in the muscles in your neck dissolve in that warm flowing light. Let all those muscles become very deeply relaxed. See that light now flowing across your shoulders, around your shoulder blades, around the middle back and down to your lower back. Let any tension in the muscles in your back dissolve in that warm flowing light. Let all those muscles become very deeply relaxed. Now see that light flowing down your arms, around your upper arms and your forearms, across your hands and between your fingers. Let any tension in the muscles in your arms and hands dissolve in that warm flowing light. Let all those muscles become very deeply relaxed.

Now see that light flowing around your chest, down around your stomach and across your hips. Let any tension in the muscles in these areas dissolve in that warm flowing light. Let all those muscles become very deeply relaxed. Now see that light flowing down your legs, around your thighs, your knees, around your calves, and ankles. Let any tension in the muscles in your legs dissolve in that warm flowing light. Let all those muscles become very deeply relaxed. See that light now flowing around your feet, across the soles of your feet and over the tops of your feet, between your toes. Let any tension in the muscles in your feet and toes dissolve in that warm flowing light. Let all those muscles become very deeply relaxed.

Pause

Now see your whole body surrounded by light. As you let go more and more, feel yourself floating in light. See that light now, filling your body, filling your toes and your feet, filling your calves and your thighs, filling your stomach, your chest, your back. See that light filling your arms, hands and fingers, filling your neck, your head and your face. If there is any area in your body where you still feel tension or discomfort, bring the light to this area. See the light flowing into the muscles and into the tissue, dissolving away tension, melting away discomfort and leaving these muscles deeply relaxed. See that light now penetrating deeper and deeper into the heart of each cell, restoring balance, creating harmony, leaving this whole area feeling very good and deeply relaxed. Let the light continue to flow around this area even when you are not aware of it, dissolving away any tension before you even feel it, so that, through the day and all through the night this area can feel very comfortable and deeply relaxed.

Now to deepen the healing process, move into an image that is very stressful. In your mind's eye, picture a huge, heavy boulder resting on your shoulders. Feel how heavy this boulder is as it crushes you under its weight. Feel yourself staggering just to stay on your feet. See the colors in the boulder. It's a big grey and black boulder. Feel your muscles, how tired they are, how tense they are, from carrying the weight of the boulder. See that deep red painful color in the muscles across your shoulders. See how the muscles are knotted with tension carrying all this weight. Be aware of how you feel. Feel the anxiety, feel the distress and be open to the intensity of this experience, as you seek to carry a burden that is more than you can handle.

Now in your mind's eye picture yourself on a beautiful sunny day with the sunlight streaming down. See this powerful white light now beginning to dissolve away the boulder. See the boulder cracking into pieces, falling to the ground. See the light dissolving the boulder away until all that remains is handful of sand. Even the sand now blows away in the wind. Just experience the relief all through your body as you stand tall. Feel the relief all through the muscles in your shoulders as they are relieved of that burden. See that white light now flowing all around your shoulders, relaxing the muscles, cooling the muscles. See that red color slowly turning to a healthy pink. Those muscles that were knotted up become long and loose. Be aware of how good your shoulders feel now, how good your whole body feels. Your head is held high. Just enjoy being out in the sunshine on this beautiful day.

Pause

Now that your body is feeling so good, choose something that you would really enjoy doing. Picture yourself in a beautiful place in nature. See what time of year it is, what time of day. As you look around you, be aware of the colors and forms and the landscape or the seascape. Feel the warmth of the sun on your face and your shoulders. As you breathe in deeply, smell any fragrance in the air. Listen to whatever sounds you can hear in this beautiful place. The sounds of nature are all around you. Be aware of how your body feels. Be aware of your emotions as they pass through you. Perhaps you feel the peacefulness and joy. Allow yourself to feel in harmony with the creations all around you. Take a little time now by yourself to enjoy fully whatever activity you have chosen to do.

Pause

Now gradually begin to bring yourself back, bringing back

with you those feelings of peacefulness and relaxation, knowing that this is a place to which you can always return. If it is time to go to sleep, let yourself drift off into your dreams. If it is time to go on with the day, gradually be aware again of your body lying down or sitting. Be aware of the room around you. Be aware of how you are feeling now. When you feel ready, you can open your eyes, and look around you. You might want to move your fingers and your toes to help yourself become fully aware of your body. Be fully aware of yourself, awake, alert, and ready to continue with your day.

"I use this guided imagery to help people manage their stress, to let go, to release muscle tension, to bring the power of imagery to confront the stress and create peacefulness and relaxation. Images of nature are an essential part of stress management."
— *Jule Scotti Post, M.S.*

12

Thumb and Finger

Guide: William J. Ronan, M.S.

The Journey

Let yourself relax and go to your special place. If you would like to be able to access this state in stressful situations, try the following:

Imagine a stressful situation such as asking for a raise, giving a speech, or whatever situation you choose. Once you have some of the feelings associated with that anxiety, then place the thumb and finger together gently. Feel the tension leave your body. Let it go as if it is draining out the tips of your fingers. Then let yourself return to your deeply relaxed state in your special place.

Repeat this technique several times, and you will find it becomes a conditioned response. Eventually the stressful situation can elicit the relaxation response automatically.

"This technique is used for any phobic, anxiety or addiction counter conditioning process."　　　　　— *William J. Ronan*

13

Window

Guide: Larry Moen

The Journey

Close your eyes and take a deep breath. Exhale slowly, letting all of your muscles, from your scalp to your toes, relax completely. Inhale again, and slowly exhale, releasing any remaining tension in your body. As you continue to breathe deeply and steadily, let your mind relax and drift gently until you find yourself standing on a white sand path.

It is smooth and firm beneath your feet. You begin to move forward. A lush tropical forest is spread on either side of the path. It is cool and shady, yet light with dappled sunshine. The white sand path ahead of you is patterned with spots sparkling in sunlight. On your right, wild hyacinths bloom in warm colors of coral, peach and fuchsia. You inhale their fragrance. Water drips from the tips of leaves, catching the sunlight as it falls through the forest.

You continue to move forward along the path. A door appears on the path a short distance ahead of you. As you approach, you notice a window inset in the door. You arrive in front of the door and look through the window. You stand and look, aware of your inner strength. You observe, understand, and feel safe. What colors...what lighting...what objects appear to you?

Pause

It is time to leave now. Turn away from the door and start back along the white sand path. You move beyond the fragrant flowers, the path still smooth and firm beneath your feet. As you walk you hear the slight rustle of the trees. You become more awake, more energetic. You feel your body again, heavy and relaxed. Breathe deeply, letting the breath revitalize your body. Slowly curl and release your fingers and your toes. Gently stretch and release every muscle in your body, waking each one individually.

Take a deep breath, exhale, and when you are ready...open your eyes.

"I use this as a gentle form of relaxation which induces pleasant childhood memories." — *Larry Moen*

Accessing the
Higher Self

14

Divine Healing

Guide: Candace T. Welsh

The Journey

Lie flat on the floor or sit straight in a chair. It is important to keep your spine straight. Now think of a smooth channel going up and down your body, relaxing it and energizing it.

As you breathe in through your nose say to yourself, "I still my mind." Think of your mind melting down into your head as you still it from the thoughts and restlessness of the day. Then breathe out and imagine your mind melting.

With the next breath you breathe in say, "I relax my body." As you say that, screen your body from head to toe, letting go of any tensions and letting your body melt downward. Now exhale with that same thought, "I relax my body."

Now take in a third breath saying, "I feel the presence of God." Now exhale and envision a presence coming to you. Feel that presence of God around you. Feel the reassuring warmth as if you are being hugged by a Divine Love.

Pause

Now release and surrender to allow the Divine Energy to come in and take over. While breathing through your nose, bring up through your feet a breath of red air. Red light flows to the pelvis area below your spine. As you inhale red say, "I let go." As the breath of red goes out say, "I let God." The next breath is orange. Breathe the orange air up through your feet to just below the navel in the stomach area. As you do say, "I let go" and as you exhale the orange say, "I let God."

Now breathe in yellow light, yellow mist, yellow air. Breathe it up through your feet, up through your legs, up to the third chakra which is just above the navel in your stomach area. Say, "I let go" as you breathe in and "I let God" as you exhale. The next breath you breathe in is green air, green mist, green light. Bring it up to the heart chakra. Inhale, "I let go." Exhale, "I let God." The next color is indigo blue, midnight blue. Breathe that mist, and light up through your feet, up to your eye-ear level. Inhale, "I let go." Exhale, "I let God." Now breathe in white light, air, and mist up through your feet, all through your entire body, out the top of your head and down your back. Now bring another one up through your feet, out of your head, and down the front of you. Now bring a third white light out of your head and surround the whole outside of you. Like a white melt down, you feel relaxed and contain a good even flow of energy throughout your body.

Pause

Bring in through the top of your head a shimmering light, a sparkle, an electrical charge. Bring it down through your head, eyes, face, shoulders, neck. Down through the arms.

Down through the chest, the heart, the stomach. Down through the legs. The shimmering light stays in your body. It shimmers up and down, back and forth, all at once. It isn't just one light beam that you direct around but many. As that shimmering light comes in it takes over your whole body. It dances back and forth, back and forth. While this light surrounds you, you feel Divine Love giving you Divine Healing now. Rest in that thought while the light shimmers around within you. Divine Love gives Divine Healing.

Pause

Your body has been recharged. The light of love and healing is the choice you made. Now it is time to come back. Let the shimmering light soften and melt out of your body. As the light leaves, affirm to yourself the great number of blessings and abundance in your life and say the prayer of thank you: "Thank you for the things I have in my life. Thank you for my wonderful mind and for my healthy body, for my loving heart. Thank you for all of the beautiful relationships in my life and thank you for all of the activities and challenging projects. I commit myself to unconditional love and self discipline."

When you're ready, wake up and come back to this room, very relaxed, recharged and awake.

"I use this visualization to relax my body and feel energy smoothly, which unclogs my body. It also reinforces Divine Healing through Divine Love." — Candace T. Welsh

15

Extended Self[1]

Guide: Maureen Murdock

The Journey

Close your eyes and begin to follow your breath in and out of your nostrils. Now give yourself the suggestion that with each exhalation, your body becomes more and more relaxed.

In this exercise you will call forth from the future your extended self. The you that has reached his (her) full potential and wisdom. Once again, open your dominant hand to receive the hand of your wise being. Feel the texture of his (her) skin. When he (she) appears, begin to interact with him (her), learning from his (her) life experience and wisdom. Notice the environments he (she) shows you. The colors, sounds, smells and tastes. You will have five minutes of clock time equal to all of the time you need to be with your extended self. Begin.

Pause

Now bring your extended self to meet your little child. The three of you sit down together; your extended self is holding

43

you, and you are holding your child. Feel the union of the three, the love and wisdom and power of all aspects of your self.

Pause

Now release both your child and extended self into their time/space dimension, knowing that you can call upon them again and that they will always be there for you.

Pause

Now become aware of who you are in your wholeness. In a moment, I will count to ten. Join me at the count of six, opening your eyes at ten, feeling relaxed and alert and ready to record your experience. One... two... three... four... five... six... seven... eight... nine... ten.

"There lives within you, your extended self, the self that has reached his full potential, your wise woman or wise man. Many people are surprised by the vivid image of their extended self, feel renewed by it, and continue to call upon this "wise being" in times of confusion or when making important decisions."
— *Maureen Murdock*

16

Finding a Personal Place[2]

Guide: David E. Bresler, Ph.D.

The Journey

Before beginning, take a moment to get comfortable and relaxed. Sit upright in a comfortable chair, feet flat on the floor, and loosen any tight clothing or jewelry or shoes that might distract you. Make sure you won't be interrupted for a few minutes. Take the telephone off the hook if necessary.

Now take a few slow, deep abdominal breaths... Inhale... Exhale... Inhale... Exhale...Focus your attention on your breathing throughout this exercise and recognize how easily slow, deep breathing alone can help to produce a nice state of deep, gentle relaxation... Let your body breathe itself, according to its own natural rhythm, slowly, easily, and deeply.

Now let's begin the exercise with the signal breath, a special message that tells the body you are ready to enter a nice state of deep relaxation. Exhale... Breathe in deeply through your nose...and blow out through your mouth... You may notice a kind of tingling sensation as you take the signal breath.

Whatever you feel is your body's way of acknowledging the developing experience of relaxation, comfort, and peace of mind.

Remember your breathing, slowly and deeply... As you concentrate your attention on your breathing, imagine a ball of pure energy or white light that starts at your lower abdomen and as you inhale, it rises up the front of your body to your forehead... As you exhale, it moves down your spine, down your legs, and into the ground.

Again, imagine this ball of pure energy or white light rise up the front of your body to your forehead as you inhale... And as you exhale, it moves down your spine, down your legs, and into the ground... Circulate the ball of energy around for a few moments. Allow its circulation to move you into even deeper states of relaxation and comfort...

Each time you inhale and exhale, you find yourself twice as relaxed as you were a moment before...Twice as comfortable... Twice as peaceful... For with each breath, every cell of your body becomes at ease... Let go, as all the tension, tightness, pain, or discomfort drains down your spine, down your legs, and into the ground... Continue to circulate this ball of energy around for a few moments...

Remember your breathing, slowly and deeply from the abdomen... Now take a brief inventory of your body, starting at the top of your head working down to the tips of your toes... Is every part of your body totally relaxed and comfortable? If so, wonderful, enjoy how it feels. However, if there is still any part of your body that is not yet fully relaxed and comfortable, simply inhale deeply sending it into the region, bringing soothing, relaxing, nourishing, healing oxygen into every cell of that area, comforting it and relaxing it. As you exhale, imagine blowing out right through your skin any tension, tightness, pain or discomfort from that area...

Again, as you inhale, bring relaxing healing oxygen into every cell of that region, and as you exhale blow away right through the skin and out into the air any tension or discomfort that remains in that area... In this way, you can use your breath to relax any part of your body that is not yet as fully relaxed and comfortable as it can be... Breath slowly and deeply, and with each breath, you find that you have become twice as relaxed as you were before, and that you are able to blow away twice as much tension and discomfort as you did with the previous breath... Inhale... Exhale... Twice as relaxed... Inhale... Exhale... Twice as comfortable...

As you allow your body to enjoy this nice state of deep, peaceful relaxation, I'd like you to think of a favorite place. It can be a real place or an imaginary place. Think of a place that's outdoors, that's beautiful, peaceful, serene and secure. A magical, special place just for you.

Experience what it would feel like to be at this imaginary place... Sense it as fully as you can... Notice the time of day... Is there a bright yellow sun, blazing in the sky? Can you feel its golden warmth beating down on your body? How good it feels... Is the sky a brilliant, dazzling blue with white puffy clouds gently floating by? Smell the air — fresh and alive.

As you sense the beauty all around you, listen to the sounds of nature as the animals and insects lazily go about their day's work... Feel the gentle breeze softly against your face, and take a big, deep breath of the clean, fresh air all around you. Inhale... As you exhale, let your rib cage collapse in total, utter relaxation. Exhale... How good it feels to be here, at one with the natural world... Enjoy it.

Look around and fully sense this place, and see if you can find a favorite spot, a place where you can sit down for a few moments to sense fully the peaceful beauty all around you... Go over to the spot and sit down. Feel the earth full and warm beneath you. Stretch out. Relax and enjoy it.

In this beautiful place in your mind's eye, you can more fully sense the interconnections of everything around you and within you... As you rest and relax, you can sense the incredible regenerative forces at work, restoring, nourishing, energizing, and healing... Take a few moments to enjoy your favorite place. It's special to you.

Pause

As you relax and enjoy how wonderful it feels to be here, tell yourself that you can return anytime you wish, simply by taking a few moments to relax yourself and by letting your imagination carry you here.

Each time you come to visit, you will find it even more beautiful, more serene, and more peaceful than ever before as new horizons are opened for you to experience... It's so easy... so accessible... so available to you.

Before leaving, tell yourself that when you end this exercise, you will feel not only rested, relaxed, and comfortable, but also energized with such a powerful sense of well-being that you will be able to respond easily to any demands that arise in the times ahead.

To end this experience for now, simply open your eyes and take the signal breath. Exhale... Inhale deeply through your nose... Blow out through your mouth... And be well.

"As a prerequisite for finding your inner adviser it is important to remove yourself from the intrusions of day-to-day life. Perhaps the best way to accomplish this is to find a favorite place in your mind's eye. One that you can visit at any time — where you can truly be yourself."   *— David E. Bresler, Ph.D.*

17

Higher Self

Guide: Margot Escott, M.S.W.

The Journey

Begin by remembering a time, when perhaps you were drifting into sleep, that state of consciousness when you weren't quite awake, and yet, you weren't quite asleep. That twilight kind of feeling. You may remember a time when you were a child and you may have had a certain dream. Many times you may have had this dream. And though you don't quite remember it, it becomes more familiar as you proceed in this journey.

You're in the room that you had as a child. It has a special door. You get out of your little bed and walk to the door. As you open the door, there is a long, dark stone staircase. It feels wet and damp, and yet you feel safe and all right with about going down the stairs. As you walk down the stairs, with your bare feet on the stone, you may feel the moss and smell the dampness of the stairway. As you continue down, you may notice that you're becoming more and more relaxed and calm. When you get to the bottom of the stairs, there is a little boat. It's a perfectly sized little boat just for you. It is still very dark as you get in the boat. You're in a cavern and as you enter the boat, it gently starts to float through the cavern. In the distance you see a speck of light that grows brighter and brighter and brighter. And as the light becomes brighter, you see yourself floating onto a beautiful calm pond in a beautiful spot in nature. The water is clear blue with a mirror-like quality to it. All around the lake are beautiful colored trees and plants and flowers. You can smell the different kinds of plants and flowers as your little boat approaches closer and closer to shore. You might hear the sounds of birds in the trees, and perhaps, an animal scurrying around. When your boat gets to the shore, it gently comes to a stop and you get out of the boat. Again, notice the feel of the soft, green grass under your bare feet. Be aware of the smells of this forest and the sounds of this place and your eyes are bathed in a beautiful green and blue and light scene of peace.

Ahead, you notice a little pathway in front of you. You begin to walk on the pathway noticing the feel of the stone path beneath your feet, aware of the smell of the trees and the flowers and perhaps noticing friendly, animals scurrying about. You notice that the path begins to go uphill. Although you're starting to go up a hill, you notice that you are able to climb effortlessly and with lots of energy, feeling totally comfortable with your body and the way that your body moves through space. You begin to go up and up this mountain path, and you turn over your right shoulder and look behind you and see, indeed, how far you have come up. You continue even farther until you've reached that place where the tree line ends. You look far, far back behind you and see where you came from and notice how small everything seems from up here. You continue walking, and although the path is very steep as you approach the top of the mountain, you still are able to travel effortlessly and easily. As you begin to reach the top of the mountain you see a cave in the near distance.

As you approach the cave you see a tiny speck in front of the cave. This speck becomes larger and larger and you begin to know that this is a being who waits for you at the top of the mountain — your inner guide. As you approach closer to your inner guide it may take the form of a man or a woman, perhaps someone you've known. Perhaps it is a representation of your higher self. This being looks at you with eyes of kindness, wisdom and love. And you see yourself reflected in the eyes of this being. What does it feel like to see yourself being looked at with eyes of love and compassion? This being has something in its hands for you. You reach out your hand and it gives you a gift. This gift may appear as a symbol, a word, perhaps a color or a feeling. Whatever it is, be open to that experience. You take the gift and you hold it in your hand and you look at it and you feel it, perhaps smell it. As you do this, you realize that this is a very, very special gift because it was meant for you — nobody else in the world but you. You take this gift and you put it into your heart and keep it there so that wherever you go you will always be in possession of this precious gift.

Before you begin your descent down the mountain, you see that the wise being wants to let you know that from now on you can access this higher self, this higher being, simply by letting yourself become relaxed and going back up the mountain. As you begin to descend the mountain you're feeling at peace and serene. Again, you travel effortlessly and easily, feeling comfortable with your body moving through space. As you come down to the bottom of the mountain, you once again find yourself on the footpath that leads you to your boat. You get back into your little boat and float back across the beautiful pond. Notice now dusk descending as the sun begins to set. You go across the pond, drifting on the water, feeling very, very relaxed and peaceful. You continue until you get to the other side and back into the cavern. Your boat rests gently by the stone steps. As you go up the stone steps, you feel again the coldness of the stone. With each step you're getting more and more aware and conscious. As you arrive at the top step and open the door you will find yourself back in a normal waking state of consciousness, feeling relaxed and at peace.

"This journey was inspired by Ilana Rubenfeld, a great teacher and healer who taught me that recovery can be gentle and full of laughter. I pay particular attention to the sensory images in this journey. If I don't understand the gift that my higher self offers me, I find that drawing it helps develop that insight.
— Margot Escott, M.S.W.

18

Inanna's Descent

Guide: Mary Ellen Carne, Ph.D.

The Journey

Find a way to make yourself comfortable. Close your eyes. Begin by inhaling slowly and deeply through your nostrils. Let the breath out through your nose slowly and completely. Continue breathing in this manner, allowing your abdomen to rise as you inhale and fall as you exhale. As you breathe, allow yourself to relax.

Allow the feelings of relaxation to spread over your body. Allow your feet to relax. Allow your legs to relax, and let your muscles lengthen. Let the relaxation spread up to your pelvic area; continue to breathe deeply. With each breath, your body becomes more and more relaxed. Allow any worries or anxieties that you have to drift off. Release them — you don't need them here. Now let your abdomen and chest relax. Let the relaxation spread to your upper arms and down to your fingers. Now let your neck relax and your head relax…. You are experiencing a peaceful state of body relaxation and are at a time and space that are different from waking reality. You imagine and see things clearly in this place.

Imagine that it is dusk and you are on a path in a forest. It is warm, and you are wearing lightweight clothes. You are walking down the path. In front of you and behind you are others, walking the same path. The path winds gently downward and crosses a small stream with a bridge over it. You cross the bridge and are met by one of your guides, a very loved and trusted person. This guide may be familiar to you already or may be someone new. It is this person who will take you on the journey of Inanna's initiation descent and rebirth and you are eager to begin.

Your guide takes your hand, and you feel a sense of contentment flood over you as though someone has painted you with a source of supportive, healing energy that mingles with your own. Your guide leads you briefly through the forest until you reach the entrance of a cave where you feel a flow of cool moist air coming from the darkness. Surrounded by a nurturing, comforting sensation, you willingly follow your guide into the cave where you stop in front of a glowing red light. A voice tells you that this is the first of seven gates that you will encounter on your descent. You are told that at each one you will leave behind a worldly attachment, a role you play, a prized possession, an emotion or feeling that you hold for yourself or another. You are easily able to choose which one you will leave here. As you do, the gate takes on a particular shape that is symbolic to you. Notice what shape it takes. You are then easily able to step through your gate and continue your descent into the cave with your guide....

Off in the distance you see a glowing orange light signifying the second gate of descent. As you approach, the light seems to envelope you, and once again you are instructed to leave behind a worldly attachment. You take a moment to decide what you will leave behind. Once you do, the symbolic shape of the next gate appears to you. You move through it with ease and continue on your journey.

The third light you see in the cave is yellow, and you are immediately surrounded by its intensity. This gate seems a little more demanding as you are again challenged to leave behind one of your earthly attachments, a role you play in your life, a personality characteristic, a prized possession, an attitude or feeling you hold for yourself or another. The decision is a bit more difficult, but you are ultimately able to decide, and the symbolic shape of this third gate is revealed. You move through it effortlessly and proceed down your path.

The fourth light is a healing green radiance that permeates your entire being and brings a sense of peace and calm. It affirms to you that you are on the right path, and when you are asked to leave another worldly attachment behind, you decide which one quickly, so that you may continue your descent. As before, the symbol of the fourth gate is magically revealed to you with your choice and you continue on with anticipation.

The fifth light is a brilliant blue spiral that encircles you with its energy and also asks you to leave an attachment behind, a possession, role or feeling to let go of in order to enter the next gate of your descent. The choice seems more difficult, but you are able to do so and feel much lighter in body and spirit. The symbolic shape of the fifth gate is revealed to you, and you once again feel the presence of your guide leading you downward on your descent into the cave.

The sixth area of light is a deep velvet-like violet light that wraps itself around you like a cloak and requests that another earthly attachment be left behind. It becomes more difficult to choose but it is possible and you do so. The shape of the sixth gate is revealed, and you slowly step through it, descending into the deepest darkness at the bottom of the cave. You remain in this darkness with your guide, accustoming yourself with all your senses to its blackness. You remain in the blackness for what seems to be a long time, taking this opportunity to just "be" because you are now free from worldly distractions and can experience for a few moments the simple essence of who you are. You find the experience of seeing yourself in your essence to be exhilarating. Take a moment to merge with the darkness and, without distraction, encounter your Self.

Pause

You now see a pinpoint of light glowing in the distance. It gradually moves closer as though it is trying to reach out to you. You sense that it is full of goodness and love, and mysteriously you see the outline of your own body begin to appear. The outline is filmy and smoke-like but it definitely has the size and shape of your body. Observe this body forming from your place in the darkness. It becomes more and more real and yet still transparent, full of air, as if it is made up of many tiny dots of light like the one you first perceived in the darkness. The white light continues to fill your body and at the same time it becomes more and more solid, more and more dense. Although it is still made of light, the dense material begins to predominate and your guide indicates that you can join with it whenever you are ready. Your essence, discovered in the darkness, easily merges with your body image and the sensation is wonderful. It is incredibly strong and calm; its energy is immense! All of a sudden you realize that it is this body shape that is the symbol of the seventh gate and by joining it, you have already gone through it and are winding your way upward out of the darkness. You continue walking out of the darkness of the cave using only a tiny bit of your new body's power.

Slowly, but with a new found lightness and power you move out of the cave, enjoying the new body and being your true Self. It feels incredibly light but grounded and centered at the same time. You take a couple of deep breaths to more fully experience this wondrous new body. It continues to feel more and more dense as you emerge until it is almost but not exactly the same as your old body.

Your path now leads you out of the cave where you are greeted by other new bodies and their guides, friends and other people who love you. You are aware of how your light radiates out to them and how theirs meets yours. Feel the joy and pleasure that this sharing of light brings to you. Bask in the energy and light that your essence and new body have drawn to you. Rest for a moment and let your new self reflect upon who you are and what this journey has meant to you.

Pause

Now if you wish, allow your guide to help you see your reason for being here, letting it come into your consciousness. Don't be concerned if the whole picture isn't clear. It is a beginning, and you will receive more and more information as your new sense of "being" unfolds. Rest in this place, surrounded by your own supportive energy for as long as you wish. Let the new found energy and light all around you merge with the energy of your new body. Let it make you feel vibrant and whole. When you are ready to return to your usual state of consciousness, count slowly from one to three, and gently move parts of your body and return to the room. Open your eyes when you wish to do so.

"I use this guided imagery in a class entitled Women and Mythology. It helps people participate in the psycho-spiritual process of finding their core Self through the symbol and imagery of ancient myth. "   — *Mary Ellen Carne, Ph.D.*

19

Keys

Guide: Janet Doucette

The Journey

Begin with mindful breathing and settle in. You see a flight of stairs. Walk slowly down the steps, relaxing more and more as you descend. Ten, nine, eight. Seven, six, five. Four, three, two, one. You are now completely relaxed.

You are walking down a garden path. It is a beautiful garden with many wild flowers and abundant bushes and trees growing alongside the brick inlaid walkway. The walkway itself is constructed in an intricate pattern. The design is complex yet very beautiful to behold. At the sides of the path grow carefully manicured shrubbery. On the other side of the shrubs, flourishes a wild and untended garden of vibrant colors and flowers of unimaginable beauty. In this lovely setting, it seems as if all seasons are contained in one. Daffodils bloom beside roses; lilacs beside autumnal chrysanthemums. This is one of many strange and wonderful aspects of this garden. Many wild creatures walk through the garden in perfect contentment. Though some animals are the natural predator of others, they walk together in peace while within this magnificent place. You come upon a wrought iron bench and sit down to gaze at the garden around you. It is nice to look upon, but impossible to enter for there is no break in the thick shrubbery and no path through the wild undergrowth.

Soon a man, who is also walking along the path, joins you on the bench. He is smoking a pipe and wearing a dark hat. He is a Jewish man, and he's wearing a beautiful chain about his neck, from which is suspended a large key made of alabaster. Begin to walk together down the garden path.

Later you come upon a Buddhist woman who is quietly praying at a small shrine set into the wall of shrubbery that borders the great garden. She completes her prayers and stands up to face you. She, too, wears a key. It is bright gold and hangs from a golden chain that encircles her waist. You begin to discuss the keys. You talk about values and aspirations, beliefs and fears. It appears you have much in common but when you begin to talk about the manner in which one ought to seek goals and how one should behave in the world, you become bitterly opposed. You agree that these differences are to be expected in a world such as ours. You walk along together each believing, secretly, your own perception of life to be the only true way.

Soon you meet another traveler on the intricately patterned brick walkway. It is a Muslim gentleman. He wears an iron key on a strap around his waist. He joins you and he and the Jewish man fall into a heated discussion.

Before long, you meet a man from North America who asks if he can walk with you. He is a preacher of fundamentalist background and is very adamant about the copper key that he carries in his pocket. You begin spirited conversations with each other as you progress along the path. Soon your discussions and your capabilities to interpret scriptures and argue logically engross you fully, and you neglect to look at the beautiful scenery before you. The Buddhist woman says very little. She stops at the many pathside shrines to intone her endless prayers and hurries to catch up with your quick-paced group of dissenters.

Eventually, the group rounds a curve in the garden and struggles up a steep hill. There before you is a valley. In the valley stands a great walled city. It is the most breathtaking city any of you has ever seen. Speechless, and with great reverence, you approach the gate to the magnificent city. By the great sliding bolt on the gate are a series of locks. There is a gold lock and an alabaster lock. There is an iron lock and a copper lock. The Jewish man slides his alabaster key into the alabaster lock, confident of results. It does not release the bolt. He removes his key. The Muslim man set his iron key into the appropriate lock and turns it expectantly. Still the bolt remains tight in its hasp. With tears and great discouragement he removes his key. The Buddhist woman places her gold key in the gold lock without hesitation and turns the key. It does not release the bolt. Sadly she removes the key. The fundamentalist preacher steps forward and gives a short sermon. He makes a great ceremony of his copper key. He says, "It is evident to me that my key is the one that will turn the lock. It is clear that my key is the only true key to this gate since none of yours has opened it." He places his copper key in the copper lock and turns it. There is a creaking noise but the bolt remains fast. "I don't understand," he murmurs, "Can none of us enter the city?" Your reply is, "You are only partly in error. If there are four locks it must require four keys together to unlock the gate." Quickly, they place the four keys in the four locks and, crowding together, turn the keys. A grinding noise is heard and suddenly the bolt draws back. Your simple wisdom amazes them. They did not see the answer for themselves. They ask you about your wisdom.

You reply, *"I seek not to be a doer of deed, but to become the deed itself. Through my personal meditations I have reached that state of enlightenment. That is all. As for the keys,"* you continue, *"We are them and as for the gate, I don't see one."*

You walk into the city through the barrier that exists only in the mind.

"I use this meditation to overcome the belief that there is only one "right way" of doing things. This pertains to many aspects of life, such as: religion, medicine, philosophy, etc."
— *Janet Doucette*

20

Soul Star

Guide: Joseph G. Spano, M.D.

The Journey

Close your eyes and visualize a star above the crown of your head, perhaps six, twelve or more inches. (The height depends on what seems comfortable.) See diamond light rays that burst forth in all directions. And now repeat this invocation of power that invokes the soul energy.

"I am the soul. I am the light divine. I am love. I am will. I am fixed design."

Now see the star come spiraling down in a clockwise fashion. It passes around the crown of the head; violet rays of light are ignited in the crown. It spirals around the brow; indigo blue is evoked. As it moves downward, spiraling, it passes in front of the throat and sapphire blue becomes manifest. It moves downward around the heart, front and back; beautiful emerald green light is awakened and pulsates in the heart. It continues journeying down and around the solar plexus now; golden yellow, like the semi-precious amber, is brought forth and spirals on down to the lower abdominal area, the sexual energy zone. Now the light is fiery orange, as in a topaz or in an opal. It spirals down around the base of the spine, the root; ruby red light becomes manifest. It spirals on downward and turns around like a comet spiraling through the center of the body, starting at the base of the spine and goes through each of the areas as it ascends burrowing a tunnel or tube of brilliant white light. It comes up through the chest, through the neck, through the head and out through the top of the crown and the star rests once more up above the crown.

Pause

And now repeat the process. The star spirals down around the crown, the brow and the back of the head; throat, front and back; chest, front and back; solar plexus, and lower abdomen, front and back; and down around the base of the spine. It turns and comes upward into the base of the spine through the center of the body, spiraling upward it passes once more through the upper abdomen to the chest, throat, head and out through the crown. Now there is a tube of brilliant white vibrating light from crown to root.

Pause

And now repeat: "The sons of men are one and I am one with them. I seek to love, not hate. I seek to serve and not exact due service. I seek to heal, not hurt. Let pain bring due reward and light and love. Let the soul control the outer form, and life, and all events, and bring to light the love that underlies the happenings of the time. Let vision come and insight, let the future stand revealed. Let inner union demonstrate and outer cleavages be gone. Let love prevail. Let all men love."

Pause

Now take your star and connect it with all the stars of all the souls that together to serve mankind so that there are interconnecting triangles of light that cover the planet. Send light and love into all the troubled areas of the world. Let love and light replace the darkness. Conscientiously think of the troubled spots in the world and send love and light — unconditional love, free of any judgments or contingencies. Now bring back the star. Send it forth to your loved ones. Let the star enter the crown of your loved ones and filter through liquid golden crystals, filling that individual with love and light. Actually visualize that person filling with the healing energy and love, manifest by liquid gold. The crystals penetrate into every tissue. Bring the star back above your own crown, then bring it down into your own crown. Take golden rays from the star and see the liquid crystal of gold and light enter into your brain and permeate your entire body, cleansing, feeling, harmonizing, nurturing. Feel yourself being overwhelmed by the energy of joy, the manifesting motion of love. Feel it in your fingers, toes, scalp, extremities, abdomen, chest, heart, lungs, throat—your entire being.

Pause

From the point of light within the mind of God, let light stream forth into the minds of men. Let light descend on earth. From the point of love within the heart of God, let love stream forth into the hearts of men. May Christ return to earth. From the center where the will of God is known, let purpose guide the little wills of men. The purpose that the Masters know and serve. From the center, which we call the race of men, let the plan of love and light work out and may it seal the door where evil dwells. Let light and love and power restore the plan on earth.

The star now takes place once more up above the crown of the head, beaming brightly, ready to serve you at any time in the future.

"This soulful exercise is decieving in its simplicity. It connects you with you higher self, and in so doing allows you to access you own wisdom, truth and innate harmony."

— Joseph G. Spano, M.D.

21

Source Connecting

Guide: Loryn C. Martin

The Journey

Visualize yourself on a round gold platform. On the floor of the platform is a button labeled The Source. Push the button. A beautiful ray of light comes on from above and the platform begins to lift up towards that light. You continue to lift higher and higher, and higher and higher. The light seems to get brighter and brighter, and you feel yourself becoming filled with more and more light and the energy becomes finer and finer.

Call forth the spiritual helpers of the light and visualize them assisting you as you move forth into higher and higher vibrations moving towards the Source of all light. Feel your desire to become one with The Source, to feel your connection. Allow your desire to lift you still higher and higher. Stop for a moment and allow to come forth into your mind anything in your life that has stopped you from feeling your oneness with The Source. It may be someone you need to forgive; it may be feelings of guilt or unworthiness. It may be a fear that you have to leave the pleasures of earth. It may be a combination of things. Just allow them to come forth.

Pause

Look at them and feel your desire for The Source to be greater than holding on to these things. Then feel your desire to let them go and see them leaving you, asking your spiritual friends to help carry them off to be dissolved into the light. Now feeling freer, feel your desire to connect with The Source and feel the platform once again moving upward going higher and higher and higher and higher. Feel and see yourself moving into more and more light *until you feel yourself absorbed by the light* and allow yourself to just be. Feel the energy in your heart expand.

Pause

At this point, feel The Source breathing you. Feel the oneness of just being. Stay in this energy as long as you like. Before coming back, remind yourself of your desire to have this energy be more and more a part of your life.

Then when you are ready, bring the energy back with you and bring your awareness back into the room. Bring yourself back gently and slowly.

"I give this meditation freely to all those that choose to use it for the purpose of connecting with The Source. I hope it will benefit many and that you prosper abundantly for your efforts. Many blessings." — *Loryn C. Martin*

22

Tree of Life

Guide: Fred Wass, M.H.S.

The Journey

During this imagery, feel free to move as you are instructed. These gentle movements will be optional, but sometimes they help a person become more integrated in the image and to deepen the work with their own body.

Breathe very gently. You are now breathing into a small seed located deep within your heart. The seed is planted deep in the soil of life. Relax. Feel the smallness of the seed. Go within the seed, explore the darkness.

Pause

Breathe. As you breathe a little more deeply now you can feel the first stir of life within the seed. Deep within the soil of earth, something is beginning to happen. There is a life stirring within the seed. Something is wanting to be born, to come anew, to live. Ever so gently, a small sprout begins to break forth from the seed. The sprout begins to grow upward to the earth, feeling the moisture on either side. Gently reach up with your fingers now, as you count one...reach up...two...reach up...three...reach up... four...reach up...five...reach up. Now take a deeper breath. As the seed is about to break forth through the soil, you can feel the resistance but there is something within you that needs to come forth. Lift up your shoulders now and push through the top of the soil. You are now in the light for the first time. You can feel the sun forming your little sprout. You can feel the wind blowing you back and forth as you begin to move your body, gently swaying back and forth, back and forth, back and forth. Now breathe again and begin to stretch forth your legs as the trunk begins to grow...up, away from the earth toward the sky...grow, growing to the ankles, growing, to the knees. Little nodules on the trunk of the tree begin to form, growing, up through the groin, through the stomach, growing, growing, through the heart. As branches begin to form, stretch out, let them grow. Breathe into the branches, stretch ever so gently, stretch, stretch, stretch. Notice the tiny little leaves they are forming. Feel the swaying of the wind, touch them, see them, see that deep green of the newborn leaf. See the delicacy.

Continue to grow up, grow and stretch through your throat. Begin to lift your head a little bit more, stretching your neck upward to the sky. From the head, the branches begin to form ever so flourishing. The leaves begin to cover the beautiful head, the trunk is now reaching up, and the top of your chakra crown is now opened. Look up into the sky; look at the clouds above. You are a part of the clouds. Earth and sky are joined. You belong here. You are beautiful. On the very crown chakra a little white blossom begins to open, ever so slowly. Each petal is beautiful, each petal is reaching out, feel...feel...feel...your fingers reaching forth, reaching upward to the sky. Feel again the wind brushing against the new petals of your new flower. Hear the rustle of the wind against all your leaves and branches...feel...feel...feel...the new life of a tree that you are.

Pause

Now you begin to feel a new sensation upon your forehead. A drop of gentle rain, cool, wet, refreshing. And then another drop, and still another drop of rain. The raindrop begins to slide down your face as tear, down the trunk of the tree. As the rain increases, the drops become a steady stream flowing down over your face, your chest, your back, your stomach, down through your legs, down deep into the roots of the very earth, the soil. In the roots, the rain begins to follow each of your roots, deeper and deeper into that soil. The water begins to mix with a light, golden sap, the vital life, the food of your new life. Gently you begin to raise the sap up, up, up into your ankles, into your legs. Feel the nourishment, the strength, breathe into your legs now. Mingle with the sap. Feel the thanksgiving and the joy of the legs, of the trunk, of the tree that you are. Let this sap flow through, around and around mixing with all the organs of your body, your upper and lower intestines, into the spine, and into the chakras moving ever so slowly. Then as you take a gentle deep breath, the sap moves into the heart; it begins to penetrate deeply. Inside the gold light of the sap is mixing deeply until you can see the bright gold color that is forming now within your heart; and throughout the life of the tree, the life of the soul. The sap moves forward through the arms, through all the branches; the leaves begin to breathe in the sap. Feel it going into each leaf throughout your body. Each of the cells are anxious to receive their nourishment and their new life. The sap continues to rise upward to your throat, liquid honeygently coating your throat. All the sore places in your body are being healed from this gentle, healing golden sap of life. Now it is moving through your mouth, you can now taste the sweetness of a nectar not known before, as it touches your tongue. You wet your lips with the golden sap. Now as the raindrops mixed with the sap begin to move up into your nostrils, you can smell this gentle, freshness of the new order and the new sap mixed together. As it moves into your eyes, you can see the crystal drops. Each drop is different. Each one a different crystal of life, the wonder, the miracle of the rain, the sap that is yours. Then as it moves into your ears, it begins to circle the inside and outside; then you can hear the little drops and the great drops. You can hear the rushing of the sap from the water. Sometimes deep within itself like a gentle water flow, sometimes just a drop of rain. Then as it moves up into the brain, it begins to go through the cells; it begins to mix with all the electro-motor organs of the brain, all the messages that are sent back and forth, all the thoughts become empowered by the sap. Gently stop for a moment to rest, to take a slight drink of refreshment from the new rain.

Pause

Thoughts that are fearful, can now be released because they are energized by a new life. Let go now of the worries, the fear, the anger; let go. Open up the brain now as it moves into the very highest crown chakra to be regenerated. The crown chakra begins to open and from your brain and your heart and soul, you sing forth. Raise your hands and sing, "hallelujah, thanksgiving, praise. I am a beautiful tree, I am a beautiful person, I am." Looking around, you see other trees, each different from you, some taller, some shorter, some wider, some thinner; each has a different geometric design; each gives glory in its own way. Each is holy by being the tree, by bringing forth its own fruit, its own blossom, its own leaves. It only has to be true to itself. Wave your branches to the other trees and they wave back in unison.

Now feel a drop of snow, cold, wet and for the first time you begin to notice that your leaves are now dropping and you are becoming bare, but it is different kind of cold, a different kind of bareness. You know that this is a time of relaxing, a time of waiting, a time of sleeping, a time for gentle hibernation. Allow yourself this privilege of letting the leaves go and just being with the snow. Gently the cold flakes begin to run down your trunk melting to ice water and beginning to cover the ground below. Now as far as you can see there are just a few leaves left in the beautiful white snow that covers the earth. Send your leaves wherever you wish — they now become of a new earth, waiting again to create a new season. Follow one of your leaves to some person you love. They see the brown leaf. It appears to be dead, but is is only waiting again to become part of their new life. Send your leaf anywhere you wish, to someone you resent, someone that has been difficult, some pain in your life. You can send a leaf with a message from your heart.

Pause

Feel the cold upon your trunk. Begin to feel the loneliness and some of the desolation of winter, but you can also see the sun that is starting to bring forth the spring. See the snow melting and gradually one by one, little, tiny leaves begin to spring forth. Once again the process of your new life begins.

So whether you are having good moments or bad moments, this is your process. It is all part of your destiny. Now stand tall again with all your leaves flourishing from the green of another spring, waving, waving, rejoicing, rejoicing, breath-ing deep, laughing, playing, being a part of the universe. You are a beautiful tree; you are a beautiful person. You are you; you are the only tree of its kind and relaxing in the beautiful tree that you are, you give thanks.

"I use this imagery to feel the dignity and connection of my body to the universe and God." — *Fred Wass*

23

White Cloud

Guide: Halcyone Therriault

The Journey

Relax yourself as comfortably as you can in your chair. Relax your jaws and your shoulders. Take a couple of deep breaths and just relax.

Let's take a short journey down to the beach. When you arrive, take off your shoes. Now, walk over to the ramp leading to the beach but stop at the trash container and deposit into the can all of your fears and anxieties. You don't need them on this journey today. In fact, you don't ever need them again.

Now you are ready to walk down the ramp onto the sand. It is early enough in the day so that the sand is cool and there are very few people on the beach. Go on down to the water's edge. Now that you are there with your feet in the water, turn to the north (which is to your right) and start walking.

Feel the gentle water lapping at your feet. It is early in the day and the sun is shining. It is warm on your head but not hot.

You feel the warmth moving down gently from your head into your shoulders, like a giant massage on your shoulders. It moves on down into your arms, on down your back. Just feel the warmth of the sun massaging your back. Gently circling over your pelvic area and all through your internal organs. Your intestines, your liver, the pancreas and the spleen are — relaxing any kind of tension you might feel in your stomach area. Now, the warmth has spread to your thighs, on down to your knees, into your lower legs and into your feet — filling your whole body with a natural warmth that is very, very relaxing. Continue walking with this light energy, that the sun has given to you. Feel it in your arms and in your legs, in your entire body. Remember that all your fear and all your anxiety has been left in that trash can. Since your feet are in the water, you gradually start feeling a delightful coolness take over your body. Just stand facing the water and enjoy the coolness and the light breeze. Now, look up into the sky and there's one, little, lone cloud up there. It's your cloud. It is light and fluffy and very full of wisdom. If you have a question, present it now to the cloud. Take time now to be quiet and see if an answer comes back to you. Just close your eyes and listen. Remember that your are totally at peace. The universe is always full of wisdom, and if we take the time to be quiet, sometimes our answers will come back to us. Perhaps the answer will come from your own heart.

Pause

Feel your own personal energy. Your body, because of the sun's warmth and the water's coolness is now in perfect harmony. You are at peace with yourself and the world. You can continue on with the day in this perfect harmony.

You don't want to leave this perfect setting of the beach but now we will turn around and head back . Don't pause at the trash can, let someone else take your troubles and dispose of them. You are a free spirit now. You are free of fear, free of anger, free of depression, free of disease, free of pain. You are full of life and energy. Peace be with you.

Now open your eyes, stretch your arms, neck, shoulders and your entire body.

"This journey is used for releasing fear and depression from my body. My body must be free of fear and depression to heal."
— *Halcyone Therriault*

Healing

24

Angel Massage

Guide: Margot Escott, M.S.W.

The Journey

This is a special experience, a time to let go and relax completely. Take a few deep breaths and let yourself go to that place where you feel relaxed and safe. When you're ready, close your eyes. As you breathe in, you breathe in a beautiful violet color, entering in through your nostrils and bathing your entire body with a beautiful violet color. As you exhale, you exhale a color that allows you to release any toxins, any anxiety, any fear. For the next few moments you inhale the beautiful violet color, bringing peace and relaxation to your body and exhale any tension or stress.

You become aware of a beautiful spirit guide, perhaps in the form of a shimmering angel. This is your special angel that has come to invite you to a place of rest and relaxation. With loving, gentle fingers the angel starts to massage the top of your scalp. Feel the top of your scalp being gently massaged with loving angel fingers, letting go of any unnecessary tension at the top of your head. Feel the massage going to your forehead, letting go of any wrinkles or lines or worry.

Lovingly and gently the angel massages your eyebrows and your eyelids, bringing peace and relaxation to your eyes, the area under your eyes, your nose, your cheeks, the area under your nose and around your mouth, perhaps allowing your mouth to relax even more and letting your tongue relax in your mouth. Now the angel gently massages your ears, lovingly caressing the outside and the inside of your ears. Now you feel those gentle fingers massaging away any tension in your jaw. So often we hold on to the jaw area. Let your jaw relax and let go. Know that as the angel massages the outside of your skin, the inside is also being bathed in a healing spiritual light. Feel the angel massaging the neck area, bringing release to the neck area and all of the muscles inside the throat.

Now feel your shoulders being gently massaged; letting go of any stress in the shoulders — the right shoulder, the left shoulder all the way down to the arms. The right arm, upper arm, elbow, lower arm, the wrist, the palm of the hand, and each individual finger of the right hand is lovingly massaged. You may notice now that your right hand and arm is very relaxed, perhaps feeling heavy and warm. Again, let your imagination take you to your left arm and feel the angel massaging the top of the left arm, the lower part, your elbow, the left hand, the palm of the hand, the fingertips. Your left arm now is very, very relaxed. Perhaps there is a pleasant, heavy warm feeling. Now allow your angel to massage the chest area, letting go of any tension and stress in the ribs inside the chest area. Feel those loving fingers permeate through to your heart area and imagine your heart area being bathed in a healing, luminous light.

And allow the angel to massage the abdomen so that the internal organs — the liver, the kidneys, the intestines also receive a healing massage. Feel the loving hand massage the buttock area, letting go of any tension or stress there. Feel the massage at the bottom of your spinal column and feel the angel massaging vertebrae by vertebrae, going up the spinal column, radiating through the entire back, bringing peaceful relaxation to the entire back area. Now begin to feel the angel massage your legs, starting at the top of the right leg. Feel those loving, tender fingers on the right hip and thigh, the right knee, behind the knee, the right calf. Feel those loving, tender fingers massaging the Achilles. And now, the ankle and the feet. The bottoms of the feet and the toes. Each individual toe receives a gentle massage, from your big toe of the right foot all the way to the little toe. You may notice that your entire right leg is becoming heavy, and there's a pleasant warm sensation through you right leg. Now feel the angel begin to massage your left leg, the left thigh, knee, calf, Achilles, ankle, foot, top of the foot, and again each of the toes of the left foot, so that your entire left leg is feels peaceful and relaxed.

If there is any area where you're still carrying tension and stress, imagine your angel giving you more attention in that area. Now be aware of your angel guiding you in positive healing affirmations, allowing you to achieve your highest good and manifest all the beauty that you have inside. "I am at peace. I am calm. I love and accept my body as it is today. All of my body is operating peacefully and uniformly." All of the blood vessels and the cells, the skeletal and the muscle are functioning as they should.

If there's any area where you need extra love and attention, give your own affirmation to that part of the body now. In a moment your angel will be leaving. Know that you can bring back the angel of relaxation and heavenly angelic massage merely by closing your eyes, relaxing, breathing in the violet color and breathing out anything you don't need right now. As we count from one to three you'll find yourself becoming more and more awake and alert, feeling refreshed and at one with your body, your mind and your spirit. One, two, three.

"So often our bodies are neglected while we focus on our spiritual journey. This imagery is particularly healing for people working on body image issues and recovering from food addiction."
— *Margot Escott, M.S.W.*

25

Body Breathing

Guide: Larry Moen

The Journey

Inhale deeply, feeling relaxed throughout your entire body with each inhalation and exhalation of your breath. Breathe in again feeling heavier and deeper. You feel your body with each breath. You are becoming heavier and more relaxed with each inhalation and exhalation. It's important to be aware of your breathing throughout this entire journey for the breathing is the journey.

Find yourself standing on top of a hill in some grass that's a foot high. In the grass are wild, yellow, small-budded flowers. You now lie down in the tall, wild, deep green grass. As you descend to the ground, you notice the grass creates an opening that separates to make room for your body. Lie flat on your back. With your face up, notice the grass all around you begins to weep forward and covers you. You are totally submerged in this grass. It's as soft on your body as silk with a touch of the yellow flowers for added color and scent.

Pause

You notice there is a figure standing at your feet. It's a figure of a person. This person wants to join you, and you allow him or her into your heart. The grass reopens and accepts this person who kneels down beside you. You spread your arms far apart, welcoming and caressing this person. The grass then covers both of you like a blanket.

You both begin to be aware of your breaths. Both breathing simultaneously, you inhale through every pore of your body. As you inhale, you feel a wave coming up through your pores from your feet. This wave begins to flow up through your body to your head and then descends back down again when you start your exhalation. The breath weaves between your bodies, going through every pore on the way down. Inhale again, through every pore, feeling a tingling sensation over the entire length of your beautiful body. From the top of your head, down through your neck, your shoulders, your arms, every pore, your chest, your abdomen, your hips, your legs, your feet. When the wave reaches your feet, you begin your inhalation, and the wave comes back again as you feel the breath through every pore, coming upward through your entire body. Continue to do this breathing and at the same time you notice the person next to you is in sync with you. You both are inhaling each other through your pores. The two of you become one. The wave of breath, comes up through both of your bodies at the same time, the same wave, up to the head. On the exhalation, the wave descends down though both of your bodies at the same time. You become united in a loving way, in a forgiving way. Anything that has happened between the two of you in the past has been released. It is of no concern. You're starting over now. As of right now you are in the present and this is the only time of existence that matters. The importance of life is right here, right now as you both breathe together through every pore of your bodies. You are in love, you are accepting and forgiving. The two of you lie quietly just breathing.

Pause

It is time to bid your friend good-bye knowing that both of you will meet again very soon and whenever you wish. The figure stands now. The person is standing at the base of your feet, thanking you for sharing your life. As it fades away, you stretch, smile, stand and notice the grass where you were laying has a certain form to it. This image has been created by you and your willingness to improve the quality of your life. You also notice that you are still breathing through the pores of your body. If you continue this special breathing through your daily life, it eventually will become a part of your existence, which will bring many good things to you.

When you are ready you may open your eyes and continue breathing.

"Body Breathing can be practiced at any time with your eyes open or closed, while walking or talking, bathing, watching TV, washing the dishes, waiting for an appointment, waiting at a traffic light or anytime at all. Body Breathing has been helpful to me in creating a new inner awareness and calmness. It's easy to do and it just plain feels good." — Larry Moen

26

Depression Uplift

Guide: Tina Tinsley, L.M.S.W.

The Journey

Just begin to relax and unwind as you find yourself sinking deeper and deeper into the chair in which you are sitting. Take a deep breath and feel gravity pull on you as you are able to just let go. Let go of all the tension, the thoughts, the old behaviors that keep you bound. Give yourself permission to step away. Leaving behind the present, for just a little while.

As you let your mind go, you discover yourself walking down a path. It is a beautiful, peaceful path. It is a path going just to where you need to go. It is a path on which you can begin to discover yourself... realizing that discovery begins with recognizing where you are.

As you walk along the path you become aware of an inviting smooth rock. One that has been warmed by the sun. One that seems just right for sitting. As you sit upon the rock, thoughts begin to come to you. Although you took a long time to get here, you are here at just the right time. This is the time for you to begin to look at your life and to visualize what you would like to be. After all, it is your life. As you sit listening, you notice shadows on the walk. The shadows begin to become a moving-picture show of your life. There, before you, you begin to see yourself moving through life. You begin to see when you began being so depressed. It was as though you took on a cloak, a cloak of heaviness. Now, the cloak of heaviness seems so much a part of you that you were beginning to think it was you. How refreshing, to now notice it is not you, but something you put on. Isn't it interesting that others have begun also to think of you as inseparable from your cloak. Will they recognize you now without it? You notice how the cloak has impacted decisions you have made and how much power you have given to a cloak. Did you perhaps inherit this cloak from your family? Where were you when you picked it up along the way? Was it when you were faced with a difficult situation, something so horrible that the pain was so great? You remember how comfortable the cloak was then. However, you forgot how to take it off. No wonder you have felt so weighted down. You had not noticed how heavy the cloak had become.

The cloak makes its presence known in your life through your thoughts. Thoughts! Thoughts that bathe you in depression, that cover you with deep blue. Thoughts that are no stronger than an early morning fog getting ready for the break of a new day. Thoughts that can be gone in the brightness of the noonday sun. Depression is held only with thoughts. Thoughts are the ingredients of depression. Thoughts, are also the ingredients of joy.

Now you hear these words: "Do not have a mind of stone, but be fluid, like the water. The water, you know, is what gave the stone its smoothness. It rounded the rough edges and gave it curves. Pay attention to the flow of thoughts. Become aware of the thoughts. They are the cloak. The choice is yours. The thoughts are yours. Joy can flood in, filling every space, ushered in upon thoughts. Be aware of your thoughts. Become a connoisseur of thoughts. Sadness is impossible without thoughts. Gladness is impossible without thoughts. Thoughts, your choice, your life."

As the speaking stops, there is silence. You notice the cloak about you. You slowly begin to let it fall. It falls gently and softly and now lays about your feet. You experience the warmth of the sun, falling upon and bathing your skin, you feel a lightness that is somehow unexplainable. Your feelings are lifted up, up and further up. You are soaring, no longer weighted down, no longer encompassed by anything but lightness, calmness, a sense of serenity. You are now soaring, new choices are yours. You are becoming aware. You can not return to not knowing. You place the cloak into your sack, glad for this experience. What you do now and the repertoire of thoughts you develop is your choice. These are the thoughts you bring back with you, as you find yourself in this room, at this time, occupying the chair on which you sit. You may open your eyes.

"It is extremely important for individuals to become aware of the conversations they have with themselves. For these conversations become the reality they live." — *Tina Tinsley*

27

Glove Anesthesia[3]

Guide: David E. Bresler, Ph.D.

The Journey

Before beginning, take a moment to get comfortable and relaxed. Sit upright in a comfortable chair, feet flat on the floor, and loosen any tight clothing or jewelry or shoes that might distract you. Make sure you won't be interrupted for a few minutes. Take the telephone off the hook if necessary.

Take a few slow, deep abdominal breaths. Inhale... Exhale... Inhale... Exhale... Focus your attention on your breathing throughout this exercise, and recognize how easily slow, deep breathing alone can help produce a nice state of deep, gentle relaxation.

Let your body breathe itself, according to its own natural rhythm, slowly, easily, and deeply. Now, close your eyes and begin the exercise with the signal breath, a special message that tells the body you are ready to enter a state of deep relaxation. Exhale... Breathe in deeply through your nose... And blow out through your mouth.

You may notice a kind of tingling sensation as you take the signal breath. But whatever you feel is your body's way of acknowledging the experience of relaxation, comfort and peace of mind that awaits you.

Remember your breathing, slowly and deeply... As you concentrate your attention on your breathing, imagine a ball of pure energy or white light that starts at your lower abdomen, and as you inhale, it rises up the front of your body to your forehead... As you exhale, it moves down your spine, down your legs, and into the ground...

Again, imagine this ball of pure energy or white light rise up the front of your body to you forehead as you inhale... And as you exhale, it goes down your spine, down your legs, and into the ground... Circulate the ball of energy around for a few moments... Allow its circulation to move you into even deeper states of relaxation and comfort...

Each time you inhale and exhale, you may be surprised to find yourself twice as relaxed as you were a moment before... Twice as comfortable... Twice as peaceful... For with each breath, every cell of your body becomes at ease... Let go as all the tension, tightness, pain, or discomfort drains down your spine, down your legs, and into the ground... Continue to circulate this ball of energy around for a few moments...

Remember your breathing, slowly and deeply from the abdomen... Now take a brief inventory of your body, starting at the top of your head working down to the tips of your toes... Is every part of your body totally relaxed and comfortable? If so, wonderful, enjoy how good it feels.

However, if there is still any part of your body that is not yet fully relaxed and comfortable, simply inhale a deep breath and send it into that region, bringing soothing, relaxing, nourishing, healing oxygen into every cell of that area, comforting it and relaxing it.

As you exhale, imagine blowing out right through your skin any tension, tightness, pain or discomfort from that area... Again, as you inhale, bring relaxing healing oxygen into every cell of that region, and as you exhale blow away right through the skin and out into the air any tension or discomfort that remains in that area... In this way, you can use your breath to relax any part of your body which is not yet as fully relaxed and comfortable as it can be...

Breath slowly and deeply, and with each breath, you may be surprised to find that you have become twice as relaxed as you were before and that you are able to blow away twice as much tension and discomfort as you did with the previous breath... Inhale... Exhale... Twice as relaxed... Inhale... Exhale... Twice as comfortable...

Now with your eyes remaining closed, imagine that a small table is being placed in front of you. On the table is a bucket filled with a sparkling clear, odorless fluid. Can you see it in your mind's eye? Is the bucket a metal or plastic one? What color is it? Imagine it as vividly as you can.

The fluid in this bucket is an extremely potent anesthetic, one so powerful that it can easily penetrate any living tissue, quickly rendering it insensitive to all feeling. In a moment, at the count of three, I will instruct you to lift your right or left hand, and then dip it into the imaginary bucket up to wrist level. Really do it, really lift your hand, for if you proceed through these actions as if they are real, you may be surprised to discover that the relief you experience will also be real.

One... two... three... Now raise your hand and slowly dip it into the bucket. Feel your fingertips tingle as the anesthetic is quickly absorbed. When you feel the tingle, or any change in your fingertips, slowly begin to dip your hand deeper. Feel the numbness go up to your knuckles, across your palm and the back of your hand, and now, all the way up to your wrist...

The skin on your hand may be beginning to feel constricted and tingly, and as the anesthetic penetrates even deeper, you may begin to notice a numb, wooden-like feeling in the muscles of your hand and fingers.

As the numbness seeps even deeper, the bones themselves may lose all feeling. Gently swirl your hand around in the bucket to ensure the deepest possible penetration of the anesthetic solution. Sense any remaining feelings in your hand moving out the tips of your fingers, floating down softly to the bottom of the bucket.

Continue to swirl your hand around for as long as it takes to achieve total anesthesia, a deep feeling of tingling numbness.

In a moment, at the count of three, I will instruct you to remove your hand from the bucket and gently to place it directly on any part of your body that hurts. This will permit you to transfer the deep feelings of numbness from your hand into the area of your discomfort, and in exchange, any tension, tightness, pain, or discomfort will flow from this area back into your hand... You will then re-dip your hand into the bucket to remove these uncomfortable sensations, and to refill your hand again with the pain-relieving numbness.

One... two... three...Now remove your hand from the bucket and place it directly on the part of your body that hurts. Imagine all the deep feelings of numbness from your hand streaming into every cell of that area, and simultaneously, picture your hand beginning to absorb all the discomfort from that area.

Notice that the same numbness that quickly developed in your hand is now permeating the painful part of your body. Can you sense the skin constricting? Are the muscles losing all feeling as the numbness penetrates even deeper? Can you experience your hand becoming filled with the uncomfortable sensations you once experienced only in that affected area?

Slowly rub your hand around the area until you feel you have transferred as much anesthesia and absorbed as much of the discomfort as you can. You may be surprised to notice what an immediate difference this has made.

Now, dip your hand once again into the bucket to repeat the exercise. Swirl your hand around in the anesthetic solution to allow the transferred feeling of discomfort to drain out through your fingertips and flow down to the bottom of the bucket.

At the same time, feel your hand react once again to the anesthetic solution, deeply absorbing it through the skin, into the muscles and bones. Once again, fill your hand completely with the feeling of tingly numbness. It will probably take much less time to achieve this state than it did the last time, but continue to swirl your hand around for as long as it takes, whether it be a few seconds, or even a minute or more.

Soak up as much numbness as your hand can hold, and when you're ready, place your hand back on the area of discomfort.

Once again, let the tingly, relaxed feelings of numbness seep deeply into every cell of the area. If there is any remaining discomfort, drain it back into your hand. Gently rub your hand over the area, transferring these feelings as fully as you can, until you are ready to dip your hand into the bucket once again and repeat the process.

Continue to move back and forth from the bucket to the affected area at your own pace. You may repeat the transfer process as many times as you like at your own pace. For each time you repeat it, you will be able to experience an even greater amount of comfort and relief in the affected area.

Each time you repeat the transfer, it will become easier and easier for you. Continue to practice now at your own pace...

When you are ready to end this exercise, simply shake your hand briskly to quickly return all the feelings to it that existed before the exercise began.

After completing this session of glove anesthesia, you may be surprised to notice that you will feel not only relaxed and comfortable, but energized with such a powerful sense of well-being that you will easily be able to meet any demands that arise.

To complete the exercise, simply open your eyes and take the signal breath... Exhale... Breathe in deeply through your nose... Blow out through your mouth... And be well...

"You can use Glove Anesthesia to help suppress any pain symptoms that you may experience. As you continue to practice this technique, you'll probably find that it gets easier and easier, and the relief that you achieve will last for longer periods of time. Each time you practice it, record how effective the technique has been. How much relief did it provide? A few of my patients have become so proficient at the exercise that now they only need to think of the potent anesthetic and they immediately obtain some pain relief. I hope this will be true for you, too.

Keep track of your progress with Glove Anesthesia by using a graph. Before beginning the exercise, gauge your Pain/Pleasure Level, on a -10 to +10 scale, and enter it on the graph. After the exercise is over, evaluate your Pain/Pleasure Level again, and chart it. The graph will provide an ongoing record of your success with this technique." — *David E. Bresler, Ph.D.*

28

Image of Wellness[4]

Guide: Martin L. Rossman, M.D.

The Journey

Begin as usual by taking a comfortable position and loosening any restrictive clothing or jewelry.... Take a couple of deep, full breaths and let the out breath be a real "letting go" kind of breath.... Imagine that with each exhalation you begin to release and relax any unnecessary tension you feel....

Allow your breathing to take its natural rate and rhythm... allow yourself to relax more deeply with each breath... allow the gentle movement of your chest and abdomen to take you more deeply inside....Invite your body to relax and become comfortably supported by the surface beneath it...

As you relax more deeply, your mind can become quiet and still.... When you are ready, imagine yourself going inside to that special inner place of deep peacefulness and concentration you have visited before... take time to notice what you see there today... what you hear in this special place... an aroma or a fragrance that is there... and especially that sense of peacefulness, quiet, and security that you feel in this place.

This is your special inner place... a place you can come to for rest... for healing... for learning things that will be helpful to you.

Take some time and find the spot where you feel most deeply relaxed, most quiet, centered, and connected to the natural healing qualities of this special place.... Allow yourself to sense the healing qualities of this place supporting and nourishing your vitality and movement toward greater wellness.

Pause

When you are ready, allow an image of you enjoying wellness to arise.... Welcome the image as it forms in your awareness, and allow it to become clear.... Take some time to notice what you observe.... It may look like you or be a symbolic representation.... What does it look like?... What is it wearing, if anything?...How does it move, how does it hold itself?... What is it's face like?

How does the image seem to feel?... Notice what this image is doing.... Are there other people, places, or things in this image of wellness?

What are the qualities this image embodies?... What is it about this image that conveys a sense of wellness to you?... Are there particular qualities that seem to be intimately connected with its wellness?

Pause

When you feel ready, imagine yourself becoming the image.... Notice how that feels.... Notice your posture, your face... especially notice the feelings of well-being you experience....

Imagine looking out of the eyes of the image.... How does the world look from here?... What is your world view?... If you had a motto, what would it be?

Pause

Imagine looking back at yourself.... How do you look from this perspective?... What do you think of this person you are looking at?... How do you feel about this person?... Is there anything you know that would be helpful for this person to know?

Become yourself again, and continue to feel the qualities and feelings of wellness within you.... Observe the image of wellness once more.... Does it seem different in any way?... Is there anything you understand about it now that you didn't before?

Is there anything that stands in the way of your moving more toward that experience of wellness in your daily life?

What issues or concerns arise as you consider this?... How might you deal with them in a healthy way and take a step toward greater wellness today?

When you are ready, slowly return to your waking consciousness, remembering what has been important to you in this experience.... When you come fully awake, take some time to write about your experience.

"This image may serve as a blueprint or goal to work toward, or may serve as an affirmation of the health and well-being you already experience. It may restore your vitality, and perhaps reduce your vulnerability to illness."

— *Martin L. Rossman, M.D.*

29

Listening to
Your Symptoms[5]
Guide: Martin L. Rossman, M.D.

The Journey

Begin as always by taking a comfortable position, loosening any tight clothing.... Have some writing paper and a pen or pencil close at hand.

Take a couple of deep, slow breaths, and let the out breath be a real "letting go" kind of breath.... Imagine that any unnecessary tension or discomfort begins to flow out of your body with each exhalation.... Then let your breathing take its own natural rate and rhythm, allowing yourself to sink a little deeper and become more comfortable with each gentle breath.

Invite your feet to release and relax any tension that may be there.... Notice them beginning to let go.... Invite your calves and shins to release as well... your thighs and hamstrings... your pelvis, genitals, and hips.... Feel your whole lower body releasing and relaxing as it has so many times before.... Allow your body to head for a deeper, more comfortably relaxed and focused state... and as your body relaxes, your mind can become quiet and still as well... easily and naturally... without effort.

Allow your low back and buttocks to join in the releasing and relaxing.... Allow these large muscles to become loose and soft and take a well-deserved break.... Allow your abdomen to relax as well... the muscles of your abdomen, flanks, and mid-back relaxing more deeply... the organs in your abdomen as well... your chest muscles... your shoulder blades and in between your shoulder blades... letting go... easily... naturally... the organs in your chest... your shoulders letting go... your neck muscles... your arms... forearms... wrists... hands... fingers... and thumbs... releasing and relaxing comfortably and easily... releasing your scalp...forehead... face... and jaws... the little muscles around your eyes.

And to relax more deeply — to become quiet in mind and body — imagine yourself in that special, quiet inner place you've visited before... a special inner place of peacefulness... serenity... and security for you.... Take a few moments to look around and notice what you see there... and what you hear in this special place... and any odor or aroma... and especially the feelings of peacefulness and safety that you feel here.... Find the spot in which you are most comfortable... and become centered and quiet in that spot.

Pause

When you are ready, direct your attention to the symptom or problem that has been bothering you.... Your symptom may be a pain, weakness, or dysfunction in some part of your body or a mood or emotions that are uncomfortable for you.... As you focus on the sensations involved, allow an image to appear that represents this symptom.... Allow the image to appear spontaneously, and welcome whatever image comes—it may or may not make immediate sense to you — just accept whatever comes for now.

Take some time just to observe whatever image appears, as carefully as you can.... If you would like it to be clearer, imagine you have a set of controls like you do for your TV set, and you can dial the image brighter or more vivid.... Notice details about the image.... What is its shape?... color?... texture?... density?... How big is it?... How big is it in relation to you?... Just observe it carefully without trying to change it in any way... How close or far away does it seem?... What is it doing?

Just give it your undivided attention.... As you do this notice any feelings that come up, and allow them to be there. Look deeper... are there any other feelings present as you observe this image?... When you are sure of your feelings, tell the image how you feel about it—speak directly and honestly to it (you may choose to talk out loud or express yourself silently).

Pause

Then, in your imagination, give the image a voice, and allow it to answer you. Listen carefully to what it says.

Ask the image what it wants from you, and listen to its answer.... Ask why it wants that—what does it really need? And let it respond.... Ask it also what it has to offer you, if you should meet it needs.... Again allow the image to respond.

Observe the image carefully again.... Is there anything about it you hadn't noticed before?... Does it look the same or is it different in any way?

Now, in your imagination, allow yourself to *become* the image.... What is it like to be the image?... Notice how you feel.... Notice what thoughts you have as the image.... What would your life be like if you were this image?... Just sense what it's like to be this image.

Through the eyes of the image, look back at yourself.... What do you see?... Take a few minutes to really look at yourself from this new perspective.... As the image, how do you feel about this person you are looking at.... What do you think of this person?... What do you need from this person? Speaking as the image, ask yourself for what you need.

Pause

Now slowly become yourself again.... The image has just told you what it needs from you.... What, if anything, keeps you from meeting that need?... What issues or concerns seem to get in the way?... What might you do to change the situation and take a step toward meeting the image's needs?...

Allow an image to appear for your inner advisor, a wise, kind figure who knows you well.... When you feel ready, ask your advisor about your symptom and its needs, and any thoughts, feelings, or circumstances that may make it hard for you to meet these needs.... Ask your advisor any questions you might have, and listen carefully to your advisor's responses.... Feel free to ask your advisor for help if you need it.

Pause

Now, mentally review the conversation you have had with your symptom and your advisor from the beginning.... If it feels right for you, choose one way that can begin to meet your symptom's needs—some small but tangible way you can fill some part of its unmet needs. If you can't think of any way at all, ask your advisor for a suggestion.

When you have thought of a way to begin meeting its needs, recall again the image that represents your symptom.... Ask it if it would be willing and able to give you tangible relief of symptoms if you take the steps you have thought of.... If so, let the exchange begin.... If not, ask it to tell you what you could do in exchange for perceptible relief.... Continue to dialogue until you have made a bargain or need to take a break from negotiating.

Pause

Consider the image once more.... Is there anything you have learned from it or about it?... Is there anything that you appreciate about it?... If there is, take the time to express your appreciation to it.... Express anything else that seems important... and slowly come back to your waking state and take some time to write about your experience.

"This imagery begins a dialogue with an image that represents your symptom. It will help you understand the purpose of the symptom and what it will take to allow healing to proceed. Unfortunately, we are not usually taught that our bodies are intelligent and can communicate with us. Symptoms are not the "enemy". They are a natural warning system."
                                                        — *Martin L. Rossman, M.D.*

30

Your Massage

Guide: Marcia L. Clark, LMT

The Journey

Pause ten seconds between each step.

★ Take three slow, deep breaths and relax yourself.

★ Visualize yourself receiving a soothing massage. Feel gentle strokes over your hair and forehead, then firm circular strokes all over your scalp, with special attention to those tender spots at the base of your skull.

★ Feel smoothing strokes across your forehead, cheekbones and along the jaw line, erasing all the tension from your face.

★ Relax further as you experience long, gliding strokes circle your shoulder joints and pull along the top of your shoulders and up the sides and back of your neck at just the right pressure for you. Feel slow firm strokes over the tight tender areas of the neck. Feel your shoulders and neck loosen with each repetition of the strokes.

★ Allow your arms and hands to relax as you experience gliding strokes up your arms undulating over the contours; then feel firm stretching strokes over the palms, backs and fingers of your hands.

★ Release any remaining tension through your breath as you feel clockwise circular strokes over your abdomen, then gentle movements rocking the abdomen from side to side.

★ Allow the tiredness to drain out of your legs as you feel kneading strokes up the front and back of your legs, followed by long gliding strokes up the contours of the legs. Feel your thighs and calves soften with each stroke, as if they are melting wax.

★ Be aware of the blood circulating through and reviving your feet as you experience short stimulating strokes along the tops, sides and bottoms of your feet, and gentle pulling on the toes.

★ Release the tension that is hiding deep in the muscles of your back as you feel firm, kneading strokes several times up and down both sides of your back. Then feel firm circular strokes down along the sides of your spine, followed by squeezing strokes on your shoulders and upper back.

★ Let go of all the stress held in your lower back as you experience firm strokes erasing the tightness over the top and sides of your hips.

★ Ready yourself to return to an alert state, feeling relaxed, refreshed and filled with healing energy, as you experience soothing, gliding, finishing strokes up and down your back.

"I am a massage therapist by trade, after massaging people all day I enjoy relaxing and visually receiving one myself."
— *Marcia L. Clark*

31

Sam & Sammy

Guide: Suzanne McGlamery

The Journey

You are safe, self-assured and in control. You are centered on the alignment of the body and aware of the illness that has temporarily invaded your body. It is time to destroy all of these bad cells. Use nature's tools to go through your body to locate and heal, with the forces of nature, the cells running rampant. These cells appear as shaded areas. See your body from above and take an x-ray of your body. Intuition and inner vision show you where the shaded areas are. The shaded areas are small dark spots about the size of a quarter. Envision your body as an ocean, wet, flowing freely. See the blood vessels in the body as rivers and streams. These rivers and streams travel from all points to feed into this ocean. Starting at the reservoir of the head you allow two creatures to come in. They are dolphins named Sam and Sammy. You see the dolphins swimming playfully and spontaneously; their bodies smooth and glistening as they swim back and forth, around and around. They travel the rivers and streams seeking out the malformed cells with their sonar. Your intuition shows them where to dispatch energy, focusing on the cells and cleansing the cells. You trust Sam and Sammy, letting go of all conscious feelings — just being with what's there at the moment. As they travel through and approach the malformed cells, they stop and surround them. The shaded area magnifies when the dolphins enter. With a beam of healing white light, they send out their zap. The white healing beam originates in their lower body and exits through their snout. Their zap quickly eradicates the cell. It lightens the entire shaded area. They jump for joy. The dolphins stay in the area until there are no shaded areas left. When they leave, they leave it clear of any malformed cells. Rest assured that, unknowing to you, their healing mission continues.

" *Imagery has taught me that we have power over our lives. It's a form of goal setting wherein I create visually what I want. I have found that the key to successful imagery is listening to the heart instead of the ego; then respecting whatever methods and symbols come up for me at the time, rather than following set patterns.*"
— *Suzanne McGlamery*

32

Star

Guide: Tony Capp

The Journey

Seat yourself in a lotus position or in a chair with your back straight and feet planted firmly on the floor, or sit on the floor against a back rest. Take a few deep breaths, in through the nostrils, hold to the count of six and let go in a long sigh. Let go of the cares of the day, the tensions, the problems.

Pause

See a star shining and glowing in the heavens — your own personal star. See it growing and getting brighter and brighter. See it starting to spiral down from left to right, getting closer and closer to you, until it comes to a point about twelve inches above your head. Take a golden ray from that star and send it down through the top of your head, down along the front of your spine, out the base of your spine. Send it twelve inches into the earth. This connects your soul star with your earth star. Now see the star spinning around your head and spinning around this golden ray. It starts to descend. It touches the top of your head, which like a many petaled lotus blossom, opens up and is energized. It continues down and around and touches the center of your forehead. Like a rosebud, your forehead is energized and opens up. The star continues down and around your head and comes to rest in the center of your throat. Your throat opens up as though it were a tulip, energized and vibrant. The star continues down and around your body and comes to rest in your heart area. Your heart opens up and is energized. It opens like a many petaled lotus blossom. The star continues around and down, touching your solar plexus. Like a daisy, your solar plexus opens up and is energized. The star continues around and down and touches the area between your navel and your pelvic bone, which is energized and opens up as if it were a tiger lily. The star continues around and goes to the area just in front of the base of your spine, called your root chakra. Like a red rose bud, your root chakra opens up and is energized.

Now, taking a deep breath, you draw that star up through the center of your body, up through the root chakra. It spirals around that golden ray, higher and higher through your body. Up through your solar plexus and your heart, and finally, out the top of your head. Your body is now glowing like a neon light — beautiful, clear white light, very brilliant. Once again the star starts its spiraling descent. As it touches the top of your head, ultraviolet rays come out of your lotus blossom forming a violet colored halo around your head. The star continues down, touching the center of your forehead where an indogo-colored smoke comes out of the rosebud and surrounds your forehead to form another halo. The star continues down and around, touches your throat and your throat emanates a sky blue, sapphire colored smoke that surrounds your throat and forms a halo. The star continues down and around and touches your chest area, and your chest area sends out an emerald green smoke for radiating and forming a halo of green around your heart.

The star continues down and around and touches your solar plexus and the daisy lights up, yellow in color and emanates a yellow scent that forms a yellow halo around your body. It goes down, between your navel and your pelvic area. The tiger lily emanates orange radiation or smoke and forms an orange colored halo. The star continues down and goes to your root chakra. The rose bud at the root chakra opens, emanating the color red, and that, too, forms a halo around your body. Draw that star up through your body from your root chakra, up through your solar plexus, your heart, your throat, up through your head and out the top of your head. It finally comes to rest about twelve inches above your head, where it forms a brilliant white light, diamond crystal star. You're now surrounded in a cocoon of rainbow colored rays. The star bleeds down some of its light and fuses all the colors and forms a rainbow of energy and a protective cocoon around your body.

Pause

There is a little mantra that is good to say at this time. If you choose, say it softly to yourself:

The sons of men are one and I am one with them. I seek to love not hate. I seek to serve, not exact due service. I seek to heal, not hurt. Let this soul control the outer form in life and all events and bring to light the love which underlies the happenings of the time. Let vision come, and insight. Let the future stand revealed. Let inner vision demonstrate and outer cleavages be gone. Let love prevail. Let all men love.

Now take your star and set it in front of you. As you breathe in deeply, you draw celestial energy through the top of your head into your heart. As you hold your breath momentarily, that energy builds up, and as you exhale, you exhale a golden ray of light from your heart that goes into your star and the star starts to grow. Pretty soon it's as large as the room. The more you breathe the larger the star gets. Very soon it's bigger than the house. The star keeps growing and glowing and extending beyond the town that you live in. It extends out beyond the county. It keeps growing and glowing the more you breathe; soon it's as large as the state you live in. It becomes larger than the continent you live on. It spreads across the oceans, then north and south. It encompasses all of the globe. The star keeps growing and glowing as it is joined by other stars. Then the star is re-energized. It's filled with unconditional love, with inner peace, with powers for healing, and with a sense of harmony and beauty for all things.

With the thought of peace, love, light, joy and compassion, contemplate the earth. See compassion spreading all over the globe like a wave until it covers the four horizons. Now allow your star to shrink down to the size of the earth. See it centering on your continent. See it shrinking down to the size of your continent. See it centering on your state and shrinking down to the size of your state. See it centering on your town and shrinking down to the size of your town. See it centering on the place that you dwell in and have it shrink down to that size. See it centering on your room and have it shrink down to that size. See it in front of you as a flowing star of energy that is filled with love, harmony, beauty, inner peace and knowledge — a conscious knowledge — of the I AM that is within us all.

Now, if there is anyone to whom you wish to send love, put him or her in the star. See that love energy flowing to him. Now wrap him in a blanket of that star and in your mind's eye, cut it away from the star so that it may be given unconditionally, without strings. If you know of anyone who needs healing, put him or her also in that star. See him healthy, doing the things he may not be able to do because of his illness. Wrap him in the star, cut it away. Give him that energy unconditionally, that he may use it as he wishes. Perhaps there is someone you're not getting along with. Put him in a star also. Wrap him in the blanket of the star and cut it away. Give him that love unconditionally.

Pause

Having done this, take your star and set it over your head. See the star raining down rainbow colored rays that not only surround your body and wash over it, but wash into your body. See those rays washing out all feelings of negativity, feelings of hatred, frustration and anger. See them washing into the ground. Be grateful to the earth for accepting it. And in its place fill every cell of your body with inner peace, with unconditional love, with healing energies, with harmony and beauty for all things, and a conscious knowledge of the I AM that is within you. A knowledge that you are a crucial part of God's plan. That you are important to it and very necessary. A realization that through you God experiences this world. Now take this time and have that rain fill every cell of your body with unconditional love and inner peace.

Pause

One you are filled with the love and inner peace, withdraw the golden ray. Send the star back into the heavens that it may be used for another day and time. Bring your consciousness back into your body, feeling it filled with inner peace, harmony, unconditional love. Very gently, open your eyes and come into the room. Smile and know that your are the beloved one.

"I use this meditation to send love to people at a distance. It can also be used for healing." — *Tony Capp*

33

Wash Away Your Troubles

Guide: William J. Ronan, M.S.

The Journey

Close your eyes and imagine that as you wash your face and hands, you are washing away all of your troubles. Imagine that the dirt is being washed away, leaving your mind and body. Imagine it swirling down the drain. See it leaving you. Imagine starting everyday this way. Let the dirt and pain of your life be washed down the drain. See it being flushed away. Imagine that when you brush your teeth, you are cleaning out   any uncomfortable words. Imagine when you wash your ears, you are preparing them to hear the beneficial things that are being said to you during the day, so that you can make the best decisions possible based on the information you receive. Imagine your eyes feeling more refreshed and seeing more clearly and precisely. Let it happen!

"Techniques such as these are very useful for people who are viewing themselves as bad people; victims of abuse or people with low self-esteem. When problems are severe, seeking appropriate counsel or psychotherapy is warranted."

— William J. Ronan

Inner Guides/Teachers

34

Bridge

Guide: Tony Capp

The Journey

Place yourself in a relaxed position, lying flat on the floor.
Take a deep breath, inhaling through your nose. Hold for
the count of six and exhale from you mouth in a long, deep
sigh. Let go of the tension. Let go of the cares of the day and
let go of the problems. One more time, inhale and breathe
deeply through your nose; hold to the count of six and
exhale in a long, deep sigh. Let go of the problems, the
tensions. Let go of control and the need to understand. One
more time. Inhale, hold, exhale. This is your quiet time. This
is your time to find out who you are.

Pause

In your mind's eye, find yourself at the top of a knoll. The air
is fresh and clear. The sun is shining overhead. There is a
warm breeze passing from left to right. You're at peace. In
front of you are several paths. Choose one and follow it.
Don't worry about the others, you will take them at another
time. The path you choose leads down into a meadow. You

pass a red rose bush. You admire its beauty, smell the roses, and pass on. Going a little way farther, you come to an orange tree. It is brilliant orange; you admire its beauty. Smell the orange in the air and pass on. Going a little farther, you come to a lemon tree. You smell the citrus in the air. You admire the beauty of the lemons and pass on. You come to a forest, all pine trees. You smell the fresh pine in the air. You admire the beauty of its leaves. You notice the sun filtering through the trees and you're at peace.

Pause

Leaving the forest, you come upon a brook, sapphire blue in color. It's small enough to step over and you do. In stepping over, you come upon some orchids, indigo in color. You admire their beauty; you smell the scent in the air and pass on. Then you pass through a field of violets, admiring their beauty and smelling them in the air. You follow the brook. It widens into a river and you follow the river until, up ahead, you spot a bridge. You head towards it. Once you come to it, you start to walk over it. Stopping at the middle, you look back on the scene and admire its beauty and its serenity. You turn and look down at the water. At your feet there are some pebbles. You pick a few up and throw them into the water. Notice how they drop into the water creating a back splash, creating ripples. That's the way you are, radiating to all you meet. Choose now carefully, what you wish to radiate. Let it be love and peace, understanding and harmony.

Walking off the bridge, you follow the path up the river with a sense of loneliness. You realize there are many people on many paths and that you all have to travel your own path alone. You're filled with a sense of peace and harmony.

Coming to a fence, you walk along side it until you find an opening where you pass through. You are filled with peace and harmony and a oneness with your surroundings. Off in the distance you notice a cliff and head towards it. You also notice there are stairs carved in the cliff. The bottom step is red, the next is orange, the next is yellow, the next is green, the next is sapphire blue, the next is indigo, the next is violet, and finally, there is a diamond crystal step. You come to the base of the stairs and start to climb upwards. With each step, you are raised to a higher state of consciousness. The first step is red, the next orange, the next yellow, the next green, sapphire blue, indigo, violet, and finally, diamond crystal. The last step leads you into a diamond crystal world that radiates every color of the rainbow. In the center of that world is a temple, a crystal temple radiating in the sun. You head toward that temple, going through the doors and passing into the inner chamber. This is the temple of your soul, where there is love and peace and harmony. You notice in the corner there is a guide, a wise man, a sage. He looks at you and your whole being lights up with love and peace. You know instantly that you can ask him any question and it will be answered. You can ask for healing, and he will show you how. Ask anything you wish; he has all the answers. The knowledge of the universe is within your guide. He guides you out into the universe so that you may be one with the source of all universes.

Pause

Find yourself back in your temple. Thank your inner guide. You may even want to hug him. Start to go out of the temple, taking with you the essence of the experience. Take the knowledge and the feelings of peace and unconditional love. Take the feeling of harmony, the energies of healing.

Go through the temple doors back into the diamond crystal world, return to the steps and descend feeling peace, love and harmony. Bring back the knowledge of how to be healed, the knowledge of who you really are. Go back toward the opening in the fence, go through the fence opening back to the foot of the bridge. Cross over the bridge, back through the forest and over the little brook. Go past the lemon and orange trees, and the rose bush. Go back on top of the knoll. From there it's only a short step back into your body. Feel yourself back in your body. Start to move your hands and your feet. Realize that you have brought back the essence of your experience. Realize that you are full of unconditional love, harmony, beauty, energy and healing. Open your eyes. Come back into the room. Smile. Blessings be upon you. Peace abide in your heart. May the light illuminate your soul now and forever.

"I use this meditation to help people find their inner guides and to give them a safe place to go." — *Tony Capp*

35

In The Sanctuary

Guide: Rev. Ernestine W. Cline

The Journey

Sit upright, comfortably with both feet on the floor. Breathe slowly and deeply, allowing your body to gently relax. Now, begin to see your breath as pure light. Breathe it into your body allowing the light to move into every cell of your body. See your physical form filled with radiant light. Now, with each breath, allow the light to expand beyond your physical form until it fills your entire energy field. See yourself in your sphere of energy. Know that you are a sphere of radiant, dazzling light. Hold that image and breathe deeply allowing that light to intensify and expand. Feel the peace and contentment that surrounds you.

Now, draw your awareness into your sphere of energy. Bring it to the center point of your sphere, wherever you feel that to be.

Now, find yourself in the sacred sanctuary of the inner temple. Feel the quiet peace that you find here. Know that you may come to this place anytime your choose.

Observe the surroundings. In silence, you sit in this healing place. Begin to enjoy all that you find there. A flowing fountain feeds a gentle stream of water that flows softly close by you. Listen to the music of the rippling waters, the whisper of the wings of a butterfly. Or, create your surroundings as you wish.

Pause

Now you become aware of an altar. You approach the altar and become aware of the blue flame that burns upon it. Kneel at the altar and place all of your cares and concerns in the blue flame of divine will and purpose. Release them and let them go. Allow your cares to be consumed in the blue flame of divine will. Sit now, for awhile in the silence. Listen only to the voice of wisdom and truth.

Pause

With your heart filled with freedom and thanksgiving you return to the center of your inner sanctuary.

Once again begin to be aware of your breath. Breathe slowly and deeply. Take all the time you need to move your awareness comfortably back to your physical world. Gently stretch your body and move only when you are aware and ready. So be it!

"This technique is for the purpose of assisting people in getting in touch with and coming to know the inner being. As one continues to use this process, the journey of the soul becomes more apparent to the individual. Therefore, after awhile, one finds that he is growing spiritually as well as emotionally."
— *Rev. Ernestine W. Cline*

36

Meeting an Inner Adviser[6]

Guide: David E. Bresler, Ph.D.

The Journey

Before beginning, take a moment to get comfortable and relaxed. Sit upright in a comfortable chair, feet flat on the floor, and loosen any tight clothing or jewelry or shoes that might distract you. make sure you won't be interrupted for a few minutes. Take the telephone off the hook, if necessary...

Now, take a few slow, deep, abdominal breaths... Inhale... Exhale... Inhale... Exhale... Focus your attention on your breathing throughout this exercise and recognize how easily slow deep breathing alone can help to produce a nice state of deep, gentle relaxation...Let your body breathe itself according to its own natural rhythm, slowly, easily and deeply.

Now let's begin the exercise with the signal breath, a special message that tells the body you are ready to enter a nice state of deep relaxation... Exhale... Breathe in deeply through your nose... and blow out through your mouth... You may notice a kind of tingling sensation as you take the signal breath. Whatever you feel is your body's way of acknowledging the developing experience of relaxation, comfort, and peace of mind.

Remember your breathing... slowly and deeply. As you concentrate your attention on your breathing, imagine a ball of pure energy or white light that starts at your lower abdomen ,and as you inhale, it rises up the front of your body to your forehead...As you exhale, it moves down your spine, down your legs, and into the ground.

Again, imagine this ball of pure energy or white light rise up the front of your body to your forehead as you inhale... And as you exhale, it moves down your spine, down your legs, and into the ground... Circulate the ball of energy around for a few moments... Allow its circulation to move you into even deeper states of relaxation and comfort...

Each time you inhale and exhale, you may find yourself twice as relaxed as you were a moment before... Twice as comfortable... Twice as peaceful... For with each breath, every cell of your body becomes at ease... Let go, as all the tension, tightness, pain, or discomfort drains down your spine, down your legs and into the ground... Continue to circulate this ball of energy around for a few moments...

Remember your breathing, slowly and deeply from the abdomen... Now take a brief inventory of your body, starting at the top of your head working down to the tips of your toes... Is every part of your body totally relaxed and comfortable? If so, enjoy how it feels. However, if there is still any part of your body that is not yet fully relaxed and comfortable, simply inhale a deep breath now and send it into that region, bringing soothing, relaxing, nourishing, healing oxygen into every cell of that area, comforting it and realxing it. As you exhale, imagine blowing out through your skin any tension, tightness, pain or discomfort from that area.

Again, as you inhale, bring relaxing healing oxygen into every cell of that region, and as you exhale blow away through the skin and out into the air any tension or discomfort that remains in that area... In this way, you can use your breath to relax any part of your body that is not yet as fully relaxed and comfortable as it can be... Breath slowly and deeply, and with each breath, you may find that you have become twice as relaxed as you were before, and that you are able to blow away twice as much tension and discomfort as you did with the previous breath... Inhale... Exhale... Twice as relaxed... Inhale... Exhale... Twice as comfortable.

As you allow yourself to enjoy this nice state of deep, peaceful relaxation, think of your favorite place, a place that's beautiful, peaceful, serene and secure. A magical, special place just for you.

Let your imagination become reacquainted with every detail of this beautiful spot... Sense the peacefulness all around you... Stretch out... Relax... And enjoy it.

Pause

As you relax in your favorite spot, put a smile on your face... and slowly look around. Somewhere, nearby, some living creature is waiting for you... Smiling and waiting for you to establish eye contact... This creature may immediately approach you or it may wait a few moments to be sure that you mean it no harm...

Be sure to look up in the trees or behind bushes, since your adviser may be a bit timid at first... But even if you see nothing, sense his or her presence and introduce yourself... Tell you advisor your name, and that you mean no harm, for you've come with only the friendliest intentions.

Find out your advisor's name... The first name that comes to your mind...Right now. Any name...

Put some food out before you... And ask your adviser if he or she is willing to come over and talk with you for a few moments... Don't be alarmed if your advisor becomes quite excited and starts jumping up and down at this point... Often, advisors have been waiting a long time to make this kind of contact...Until now, your advisor has only been able to talk to you sporadically through your intuition... Tell your adviser you're sorry you haven't listened more in the past, but that you'll try to do better in the future...

If you feel silly talking in this way, tell your advisor that you feel silly... That it's hard for you to take this seriously... But if you sincerely want your advisor's help, make that very, very clear... Tell your advisor that you understand that like in any friendship, it takes time for feelings of mutual trust and respect to develop...

Although your advisor knows everything about you — since your advisor is just a reflection of your inner life — tell your advisor that you won't push for any simple answers to important questions that you may be dealing with... Rather, you'd like to establish a continuing dialogue...So that anytime you need help with a problem, your advisor can tell you things of great importance... things that you may know, but you may know their significance...

If there's a problem that's been bothering you for a while, ask your advisor if he or she is willing to give you some help with it... Yes or no... Your advisor's response is the first answer that pops into your mind...Pose your questions as you exhale... And the first response that comes into your mind as you inhale is your advisor's reply... It's an inspiration... Ask your questions now.

Pause

What did your adviser reply?... Ask any other questions that are on your mind...

Pause

Continue this dialogue for a few moments...Asking your questions as you exhale... And listening to the response that pops into your mind as you inhale...

Pause

Remember, your advisor knows everything about you, but sometimes — for a very good reason — he or she will be unwilling to tell you something... This is usually to protect you from information you may not be ready to deal with... When this occurs, ask your advisor what you need to do in order to make this information available to you... Your advisor will usually show you the way...

Pause

If there is something that you'd like your advisor to be thinking about between now and the next time you meet, tell this to your advisor now...

Pause

If there is anything your advisor would like *YOU* to think about between now and the next time you meet, find out what that is...

Pause

Set up a time to meet again... A time that's convenient for you and a time that's convenient for your advisor... Be specific as to exact time and place... Tell your advisor that although these meetings are important to you, part of you is lazy or reluctant to follow through...

One way your advisor can help motivate you to continue meeting periodically is by giving you a clear demonstration of the benefits you can gain... A demonstration so powerful that you will be moved to work even harder in getting to know yourself... If you are in pain, for example, ask your advisor if he or she is willing to help motivate you by taking away that pain completely... Right now, just for a few moments, as a demonstration of power... If so, tell your advisor to do it... now...

Pause

Notice any difference?... If you're willing to do your share of the work, by relaxing yourself and meeting periodically to set things straight, there's no limit to your adviser's power... Ask for any reasonable demonstration that will undeniably convince to you of this power...

You might be, for example, somewhat forgetful... And although you want to continue these meetings with your adviser, you might forget the exact time and place that you agreed to meet... If so, ask your advisor to help you by coming into your consciousness just a few moments before it's time to meet, to remind you of the meeting.

Before leaving, tell your advisor you're open to having many different kinds of advisors... And that you will leave this totally up to your advisor's discretion... If your advisor wants to bring other advisors along the next time you meet, fine... Is there anything your advisor would like you to bring along with you the next time you meet?... If so, find out what that is...

Pause

See if your adviser will allow you to establish physical contact... This is very important... Just about every animal on the face of the earth loves to have its face stroked and its back scratched... See if your advisor will allow you to make this contact now...

Pause

While making this contact, find out if there's anything else that your advisor would like to tell you... If so, what is it?...

Pause

Is there anything that you would like to tell your advisor before you leave?... If so, do it now...

When you are ready, take the signal breath to return from this meeting... But before you do, tell yourself that each time you make contact with your adviser the communication will flow more and more smoothly... More and more easily... More and more comfortably... Tell yourself that when this experience is over, you will feel relaxed, rested, and comfortable, as well as energized with such a powerful sense of well-being that you will be able to respond easily to any demands that arise. To end this exercise, simply open your eyes and take the signal breath... Exhale... Inhale...Breathe in deeply through your nose... Blow out through your mouth...And be well.

"This guided imagery exercise will help you to make contact with an inner advisor who resides in your mind's eye. The advisors that people create are able to search the inner recesses of the unconscious mind.

When I was first introduced to the advisor technique by Dr. Irving Oyle, I was as quick to challenge it as anyone. I have been surprised at how receptive most pain sufferers are to the technique.

My patients have created advisor "playmates" like Rocky the dog, Mary the tiger, Pitu the bird, Bambi the deer, and Charlie the white rat. These imaginary creatures have helped them to accomplish what many doctors thought was impossible — a life free of agonizing pain." — *David E. Bresler, Ph.D.*

37

Mother Earth

Guide: Janet Doucette

The Journey

Begin with mindful breathing and settle in, relaxing and opening all chakra energy centers. You are walking down a hallway. At the end of the hallway there is a door. Spend a moment to notice the door, its color and the shape of the door handle. Open the door. There is a flight of stairs. Walk slowly down the steps. Ten, nine, eight, seven, six, five, four, three, two, one. You are now standing on a sandy beach. There is a mist swirling around you. It is a safe and comfortable beach. While in this mist, you may change to a more comfortable form. You may change clothing. Your hair may become longer or shorter. You may find yourself wearing ornaments or jewelry of another culture. Spend a moment to focus on the style or form that you have chosen.

Pause

You are comfortable and peaceful in your chosen form and the mist is diminishing now. As it clears, you see before you a high stone wall. There is an open gate in the stone wall through which only you can pass. It is the gateway to a magnificent and eternally blooming garden. Walk through the gateway and experience your personal spirit garden, where everything you plant grows and continually blooms or bears foliage. There is a bench in this garden. It may be wooden, wrought iron, or of stone. Please sit on this bench and look around you at the beautiful garden of your spirit. Take note of the plantings, their essential order, or their random wildness. Notice what you have planted and where. You may hear water falling from high rocks or you may have a pool or river running through your garden. This magical place of peace and symmetry is of your creation. No one may change a thing here, and no one may enter against your wishes. Take a few moments to recognize your spiritual place of peace and contentment.

Pause

Now that you have fully visualized your garden, see a Being enter. It may be an animal or person, a bird, or some mythical creature that has come to guide you on your quest. See the creature fully and greet it. Let it greet you in some manner that it may choose. There is absolutely nothing to be afraid of in this place or from this Being. It only wishes to help you. By guiding you on this journey, it will impart protection and knowledge. It will prevent any fear from opposing your chosen pathway. And now you are joining your spirit guide. You walk together, out of the familiar garden and into the forest that surrounds your special place. There is a well-worn path that leads through the forest and soon you come to a place where the pathway forks. You take the side path that begins to lead to lower elevations. You step out of the cover of the high trees and see a deep chasm with high stone cliffs on either side. You step to the edge of this cliff and look below. There is swiftly rushing water at the bottom. And there is a narrow pathway cut into the side of the cliff leading down the chasm to the river below. Your guide indicates that you should follow, and he leads you down the narrow, rock strewn path, pointing out finger-holds and tree roots that are there to help you descend. Follow the guide, now, down this treacherous but exciting path.

Pause

The sound of the raging water is loud now. So loud you cannot hear your guide speak. He can only communicate the direction to go by pointing. You are walking carefully on the rocks that border this river. It splashes wildly over the rocky elevations and sprays cool river water into your face and onto your body. It is a cleansing, refreshing coolness that makes you feel at one with the mighty river which courses defiantly and courageously on its chosen course. You absorb its power to amplify your own, strengthening your intent and firmly assured that your pathway is meant for you, as is the course of the river meant to the spirit that engendered her raging waters.

Your guide indicates a cave now. You see that there is an overhang that is wet with moss and dripping spring water. The rocks are slippery and you are careful of your step, but assured of your ability to remain in balance. In fact, you are quite aware of your increased sense of balance and your sure step. It's as if you are a dancer performing a well-known ballet. Your movements are graceful, yet determined. You feel sure of your presence and the need to carry on. The cave is long and deep and soon you find yourself in an under-ground cavern. The sound of the river has long since been muffled away and all you can hear is the steady dripping of water from the cavern roof. Droplets that are concentrated with minerals form long stalactites on the roof of the cavern.

The guide leads you past a pool of clear water and the shadowy cavern is illuminated by some glittery source of light high on the roof. A closer look reveals crystals jutting out of the rock walls, crystals that are glowing with a warm light. In the back of the cavern is a dark tunnel, and your guide indicates that you should go in first. You will have to crawl, but your guide will be right behind you. You do not question this and you are not afraid. You know that what you seek is at the other end of this tunnel, and so you begin by getting down on hand and knees. You crawl through the tunnel.

Pause

You have come to a small, well-lit cavern room. You stand up and brush yourself off. Before you stands a woman. She may be old or young. She may be radiant or she may appear wrinkled and shriveled with age. Visualize her clearly.

Pause

She looks you over critically. She walks around you and then around again. You see a smile of approval on her face and you feel her intense acceptance. She hugs you to her breast. Suddenly, you no longer feel the boundaries of a body between you. She is sharing with you the beating of one heart. You feel the inner glow of your spirit grow and expand. You see it as encompassing all the earth. You begin to see the world as she does: one magnificent moving body of fluid beauty — trees and lakes, mountains and oceans, jungle rain forests that cover an entire land undisturbed — all radiant and sustaining thousands of forms of life. She shares with you her vision of the earth from the vantage point of her sister, the moon. The world is an eerily glowing orb of a planet, illuminated by the sun, swirling with clouds, blue waters, and green verdant lands — all bearing and sustaining life, all giving birth to new living spirits moment after moment. These new physical forms will carry on her magnificent living and breathing self as one pulsing, radiating form of conscious spirit made so by her special children, mankind. Her gifted, beloved children who carry the knowledge of power, love, intent, and manifestation of spirit. Each and every one of her millions of living children are gifted with a special quality of spirit, wrapped in a precious form, and birthed into the world to heal and bring forth her message of love and communion.

Now she backs away from you, and you feel again the boundary of physical form. She tells you that you are her beloved child, that she is always with you and always within you. She is whispering that she created your spirit with a unique quality; you must find that quality and recognize it fully and with clear intent. You are more than the sum of the power animals that guide you and share their medicine with you. You are, like they, gifted with the power of silent knowledge. It is up to you to find the medicine which you ARE and when you do, you must LIVE it. You understand her to mean that when you find it, you will not reject its potent force anymore than the river can resist its course. You comprehend fully that you will instantly begin to live your life in the fullest expression of that medicine gift. In this manner you will listen to her guidance and you will be in her constant thoughts. You will see her intent in the directions of the wind, and in the flight of her winged ones. You will know her ways and keep them. Balance, harmony, beauty, birth, strength. Happiness, labor, weaving form with thoughts. You will join hands with her other children to encircle the living earth with a powerful glowing aura of the combined light of all that lives and join with her and with him in all that is. She indicates now that you should go to her cavern altar and choose a remembrance of this covenant between you and her. On the stone altar a candle is burning brightly, and it illuminates the little gifts that are strewn there. There is a feather, a stone, a bird's egg. There is a brilliant crystal, a book, and some bleached and weathered bones. There are many other objects there. Take what sings to you.

It is time to take leave and you may wish to hug her or kiss her good-bye. She whispers gently in your ear a special message, for she has known you before you were born into the world. She cradled your spirit on her breast and it will be to her vast arms that you will return when your form no longer serves you.

Pause

You see your spirit guide now standing by the altar. She is his mother as well and he honors her. She reminds you of your promise to her and she releases you. It is time to leave. The guide walks with you to an opening in the cave wall. Through the opening you walk into the clear light of day. You find yourself on the other side of the raging river. A bridge, which was not there before, beckons you. It is a special bridge constructed for only you to cross. You cross and hurry up the chasm pathway. You climb swiftly with no fear of falling and reach the top in no time at all. Your guide must run to keep up with you. Soon you are in your garden, feeling refreshed, illuminated and full of purpose. You say good-bye to your guide and disappear through the gateway into the mist. Take some time to change visually in the mist, becoming as you are in form. When you are ready, flex your wrists and feet and come back to the room. Welcome back!

38

Safe Place

Guide: Pamela M. Fox, M.S., LMHC

The Journey

Begin by relaxing into an even breath, in and out of your body, releasing tension as you exhale. Allow yourself to do this several times.

Imagine yourself walking down a long path. As you walk down this path, look around you and notice the trees. Can you smell any fragrance? How does the ground feel under your feet? Pick up some leaves, needles, pine cones, stones, or whatever you find as you're walking. Take a long, slow, deep breath, smell the air and notice whether the air is cold or warm as it is entering your nose, throat and lungs.

After a while you come to a clearing — look around — notice if there is a structure. Is it a building, cabin, cave or any other natural structure? Look for openings as you begin to investigate this safe place. Again use all of your senses to create this place for yourself.

Pause

Now slowly enter and begin to look around. Are there any furnishings in this environment? Are there pictures on the wall or any unusual objects? Is there anything familiar here that may allow you to feel safe, secure and connected to your inner guide? Allow your guide to manifest in whatever form it needs to take. If you have any questions at this time — pose them to your guide. Then be silent for a while to allow your answers to come.

Pause

If there are no answers at this time, just be aware over the next few days for responses in the form of people, books or thoughts.

Now gently bring your awareness back to your breathing and begin to come back down the path. Hear the sounds around you and slowly allow your consciousness to be brought to your current reality. Remember you can go to this place any time you need to be centered.

"I've used this journey to get in touch with my inner guides and to feel a sense of security and safety despite the stress around me."
— *Pamela M. Fox*

Receiving Gifts and Love

39

Astral Travel

Guide: Chrystle Clae

The Journey

Find your comfortable spot. Begin to breathe deeply. In through your nose, slowly; hold to the mental count of five. Even slower, exhale every bit of air before repeating these deep breaths another four times until you next hear my voice.

Pause

Continuing to breathe deeply and imagine you're in secluded woods. Springtime is awakening all of nature. Hear the birds sing their song of love to each other. Watch them tease each other, flying from one tree limb to another above you. See them flit from one tree to another several times before they actually touch. Watch this loving game. You're walking on a soft, dirt path and you can feel the comforting warmth of the earth beneath your sandaled feet. Breathing deeply, off to the left you see two cuddly rabbits nose to nose enjoying the closeness of each other. Notice the softness of their fur if they allow you to pet them. Feel the warmth they send to you and know that they feel your love just by your presence. Just beyond these rabbits, a little further down the

140

path and off to the right, is a small clearing where a soft blanket of your favorite color has been laid out for you over a soft patch of lush grass. You're in a fresh, springtime meadow, continuing to breathe deeply. Imagine you can smell the sweet and pure air. As you lie on the blanket, a cloud above you begins to move slowly, allowing your feet to be basked in the warm relaxing rays of the sun. The warmth travels gently up your legs, loosening any tense muscles. Steadily this warm, soothing feeling relaxes your knees, relaxes all of the muscles in your thighs. The warmth of the sun travels to your hips and the trunk of your body. You relax so deeply that your body seems heavier and unwilling to move. Breathing deeply and comfortably, your shoulders and upper arms feel completely at ease. The warm sun kneads you and massages your forearms, hands and fingers. The sun's growing energy relaxes all of the tensions in your neck, your jaw, and your mouth. Your cheeks relax, your ears and nose relax, and you release all the tensions. The muscles around your eyes release all tenseness and your forehead relaxes. You're completely relaxed. Feel the tensions leave the back of your head, all the way to the crown of your head. Your whole body is relaxed and at ease, and you continue to breathe deeply. Exhale slowly.

You look above you and see a golden ball of energy coming towards you from the sky. As it approaches closer, you feel that this ball of energy is a protection and a traveling vehicle for your spirit. Your body lies peacefully, heavy, and unwilling to move on the soft blanket in the grass. As this golden ball approaches, your spirit slips out through the top of your body. You look back and see your body lying on that blanket, peaceful and relaxed. The door opens in this sphere of gold. Inside this door is a being of light. Look into the eyes of this light being and instantly feel the peace, the love and the protection that this being offers you. Telepathically this being gives you the message that you have nothing to fear and that this vehicle is here and you can just soar beyond the stars and visit those stars and the planets. Your light-being guide tells you that you have wonderful experiences ahead of you and reaches out its hand to guide you into this golden sphere. As you sit down, on a comfortable seat inside, the magical door closes, and you're instantly taken up into space.

Watch as the stars and colors whirl by you. You feel so at peace, so happy, so loved. You sense that you are rising and floating. Now slowly, gently, so very safely, know that you're protected by love from this beautiful light being. Holding this being-guide's hand you realize that you're no longer in a vehicle, but you're floating, drifting and gently bobbing along like a cork in a pond. As you drift, drift and float higher, you glance easily down towards the earth. You know that you have the ability to travel anywhere you wish, instantly. You have but to think of a location, and you'll be there. The light guide suggests that the first stop is Venus. You slowly descend to this planet knowing that the atmosphere is comfortable and very relaxed for you. As you touch ground you sense a soft, pink vibration all around you. It's a vibration of love. Now, look ahead and see someone coming towards you. You instinctively know this is your master teacher, clothed in a white, flowing gown. As your master teacher comes closer, you see the wisdom in the eyes; you see the love in the eyes. As your master teacher opens those loving arms you walk towards him or her and feel the embrace. This is a teacher who loves you as you are, from the very beginning; with no judgements. This person knows how special you are and tells you. Your teacher understands that life on earth isn't always easy, but anytime you feel the need for a reinforcement of love and understanding, your teacher is most happy to see you. You see the tears welling in the teacher's eyes. You feel the love.

Look around you and see that the pink, cloud-like vibration has changed to a crystal city where everyone around you radiates unconditional love. As you walk on this cool marble floor, everyone you pass has a smile and a feeling of understanding. Continuing to breathe deeply, look around and see if there's anyone you know also visiting this planet of Venus. You now realize that you're here for a lesson. You're here to come to school. You approach a classroom, walk through the door, and sit down in a comfortable chair. Your master teacher is there, ready to begin the lesson. Look around you at the other students. There's probably someone there that you know. Now, take a moment and listen to the lesson. Sense what you're being taught.

Pause

Now sense how you can use this lesson in your earthly life when you return. Each of you is there for a reason, a specific purpose, to enhance all life on earth in your own subtle way.

Instantly your light-being friend and guide is once more by your side. With outreached hands you join, and begin to float once more. Up and up, higher and higher. Your light-guide tells you that this time you're going to visit the planet Neptune. As soon as the name is said, you begin descending, touching ever so slowly and lightly, to the planet Neptune. Immediately you sense a soft, violet vibration. You're immersed in it. You breathe it in. You feel it around you. Ther are no visible beings on this planet. This is a planet of solitude, of comfort, of peace and tranquility. This is a planet of depth and understanding. With each deep breath that you take, the soft, violet energy changes your being, your inner being — the real you. Even in your spirit you feel the area between your eyebrows stimulated. Feel it vibrate with each deep violet, soft breath that you take. It massages your third eye area. Now, be aware of the myriad of colors that flash before your eye, your inner eye. Almost like fireworks, you see them. Your inner vision is enhanced. Your ability to visualize has progressed immensely. Taking more deep breaths of this soft violet energy of the planet Neptune, your spiritual senses awaken. You know that you have a keener ability to see into your future, to see into others' futures when it's for their greater good and gain. When it's for your greater good and gain. When it's productive and right, you're able to sense others' problems and solutions that you can share and know will be accepted with open minds and hearts because you're giving them total love without judgement, without sanctioning. Anything you see, perceive or feel is for the betterment of those it concerns. Take another deep breath of the soft violet vibration and know that you can come back here anytime to reinforce these psychic abilities, these extra perceptions that the planet Neptune enhances.

Once more the light being appears beside you. Holding this being guide's hand, you decide to travel back to Earth still in your spirit. You want to be with someone who you care about. Visualize this person, this loved one, and immediately you're beside that person. You know instantly where this person was and now you see this person clearly before you. See clearly the eyes, the nose, the hair, the face of this loved one. Know with complete certainty that you really are there beside this special person. You can't touch this person, but you can project a mental message. Project the warmth of unconditional love. The person won't be aware that you're sending the message but will feel and sense the meaning. Now, send a special message that you'd like to convey to this special person.

Pause

Your light-guide comes back, takes your hand once more, and slowly guides you to the place where you left your body, nestled on that blanket on the grass. Before you re-enter your body, your guide telepathically assures you that you can come back to this spot in the grass where he or she will meet you to go to further adventures, anywhere you'd like, anytime you're ready. You'll have the ability to move wherever you like. Nothing will ever harm you or distress you. Now, gently and slowly, relax into your body. As you enter, feel your body take a deep breath. Still and completely comfortable and released, begin to wiggle your toes and fingers. Breathing deeply, comforted, totally at ease. As I count backwards from five to one, begin slowly to fully awaken. Five, breathing deeply. Four. Be aware of all the sensations in your body. Three, awakening slowly, completely refreshed and relaxed. Two, breathing deeply, filled with the love that you experienced on Venus. One, slowly open your eyes at a pace that's comfortable for you. You are filled with a new sense of awareness, a new sense of unconditional love for all living things, a feeling of lack of prejudice, lack of judgement, total acceptance in life. You to see the best in all that there is.

"Thank you for choosing to grow in this way. You've enhanced the entire world by making this step. My wish for you from this point on in your life is for you to be filled with peace, light and a real sense of being loved and loving unconditionally."
— *Chrystle Clae*

40

Lotus Flower[7]

Guide: Maureen Murdock

The Journey

Close your eyes and focus your attention on your heart, or the area in the middle of your chest. Imagine there is a closed golden-petaled lotus flower. As you breath into your heart, the energy from your heart slowly open the petals of the lotus flower.
Pause
And a beautiful blue light emanates from the center of the lotus flower. You have all the time you need to open your flower.
Pause
As the lotus continues to open, the blue light expands, filling you with love and light.
Pause
Notice how the blue light from your hearts joins with the light from the hearts here present.
Pause
Now let that image go, notice how you feel and slowly open your eyes, feeling fully alert, yet very relaxed.

41

Receiving Gratitude

Guide: Majorie Michael Munly

The Journey

Sit comfortably, or lie down, allowing your whole body the well-deserved opportunity to relax. Take a slow deep comfortable breath in through the nose, then, out through the mouth. Repeat this five times.

Pause

Next allow your attention to go to each area of your body beginning with your feet. Feel each bone, muscle and joint become very heavy. Your whole body knows that it can let go of any effort.

Imagine that you are about to embark on an effortless journey to a place where you feel safe, at home and at peace. It can be at the beach, mountains, forest or a place remembered from childhood... perhaps even a home or favorite childhood room. Notice the sounds, smells, charm and unique beauty here. They nourish your senses. You are totally supported and at peace.

Reflect back on your life thus far – that is– bring to the front of your memory those people whose lives you have touched in some way by caring, by supporting, by nurturing, by teaching, . One by one a loving, familiar face comes before you, expressing a heart felt thank you for what it is you have given..

Pause

Notice what it is each person has to say. As each expression of gratitude is given, receive it into your heart and mind as truth.

If at any time you wish to be reminded of what you have given, you may call to mind what you have seen and heard here today.

"This guided imagery will enable its user to remember and claim contributions made to the lives of others. It is especially useful for parents or those in service professions who in evaluating themselves, never seem to do enough for others."
— *Marjorie M. Munly*

42

Rose Pink Bubble

Guide: Karen M. Thomson, Ph.D.

The Journey

Completely and totally relax as you begin to breathe slowly and deeply. With every inhalation, know that you're breathing in oxygen, energy, Light, and all that's positive; so breathe in slowly and completely fill the body. As you breathe out, exhale completely, and know that you are letting go of toxins, frustration, anxiety, darkness, and anything you no longer need. Completely and totally exhale, just as you completely and totally inhale. Keep your concentration on your breathing, as both the inhalation and the exhalation are equally important and equally slow, deep, and complete.

With your eyes closed, take a slow, deep breath, and feel your body relaxing from the top of the head, down your scalp, facial muscles, neck, shoulders, down the arms, and out the finger tips. Continue slowly and deeply breathing...Again, return your awareness to your body, and feel the deep relaxation moving now from your shoulders down your chest, down your spine, down your stomach area, hips, legs, knees, calves, ankles, feet, and out the toes. Now see your entire body filled with Light and Peace and all that is positive, and as you inhale, breathe in Light and energy, and feel now an even greater state of relaxation. Check out your body: if there is an area of the body where there is discomfort or dis-ease, focus the Light and the Peaceful, Loving, Healing energy there, and see the Light absorbing any pain, discomfort, or darkness. Again, take a deep breath and see the body filled with and surrounded by a most beautiful, peaceful, and loving Light, which now extends several feet from the body. See the body now as surrounded in a cocoon of rose pink Light. You feel as though you are immersed and bathed in pink Light, and as you breathe in deeply, you inhale — drink in — this beautiful pink Light that is now filling and surrounding your body. You are feeling completely peaceful and relaxed, and have a wonderful sense of well-being. In this rose pink bubble of Light, you have the awareness, the knowing that you are completely loving and totally, unconditionally loved. Stay in the rose pink bubble as long as you like, and bask, bathe in its Light. When you're ready to come out of it, simply open your eyes. You can recall the sense of deep well-being and relaxation and the feeling of total love at any time simply by remembering this experience in the rose pink bubble.

"I use this both alone in my meditations and also during my yoga and meditation classes, usually with soothing background music, to assist with a greater sense of well-being and the feeling of being loved and loving unconditionally."

— *Karen M. Thomson, Ph.D.*

43

Treasure Chest

Guide: Gail Nicholas Magruder, M. Div.

The Journey

Take your shoes off and place your feet flat on the floor. Be comfortable. Close your eyes. Breathe deeply guiding the fresh breath of air to any parts of your body that are tense. Breathe into them. Imagine the tension draining away through your arms and legs. Breathe deeply and slowly. Breathe in to the count of eight, pause, then breathe out to the count of ten. Being gentle with yourself, leave your head and go to your inner sanctuary, your heart space.

You are about to go on a journey into the woods. You are walking along a trail lined with towering pine trees. Shafts of sunlight shimmer on the ferns along the way. You are aware of soft air, birds singing, and the smell of the pine needles.

Suddenly the woods open out, and there in front of you is a large field. Daisies dance in the soft breeze. The sun is warm on your back as you walk to the middle of the clearing. You sit down on the meadow grass and soak in the sun. Insects dance around you. Clouds float by. You notice a rock nearby that has some letters cut into it. You move closer and; just make out the words, "Where your treasure is, there will your heart be also."

You roll the rock away. Then with your hands, you begin to dig into the earth. Your heart is pounding. You know there is a treasure – your treasure – hidden in the ground. You uncover a battered tin box. Using a stick you force open its top. There inside, you behold your treasure. You gaze in rapt attention, taking in its beauty and richness. You are filled with unspeakable joy. It permeates your whole being. Minutes, hours, pass without notice. You are lost in the wonder of your treasure.

Pause

At last you slowly turn, replacing the treasure box, and walk back across the field into the woods. On the trail home, you glow with the memory of what you have just seen. You know the treasure is yours to carry in your heart.

"This meditation allows each person to "SEE" – to discover – what his or her spirit "needs" to see in the box. It is a grounding meditation that draws us back into nature, into our connection with God's creation." — *Gail Nicholas Magruder*

Training and Control

44

Concentration-Retention -Total Recall
Guide: Richard J. Palmer

The Journey

Fix your eyes on a spot on the ceiling overhead, just pick out an imaginary spot and stare at the spot without moving a muscle. Now take a deep breath and fill up your lungs, exhale slowly, sleep now. Now a second and even deeper breath, exhale, sleep now and now a third deep breath, exhale, sleep now. Now let your eyelids close. As each muscle and nerve begins to grow loose and limp and lazy all of your cares and tensions fade away. You are relaxing more with each sound you hear, with each easy breath that you take. You are going deeper and deeper into drowsy relaxation.

I am going to count from ten down to one and as I do I want you to picture and imagine that you are walking down a flight of steps. With each number that I count, the quality of your deep relaxation becomes more profound and more intense. When I reach the count of one you will then be aware that you are enjoying a very healthful, very pleasant state of hypnotic relaxation. Number ten we take the first step downward, each muscle and each nerve grows loose and limp and relaxed. Number nine the wave of relaxation spreads all across your body. Number eight you're relaxing more with each easy breath that you take, with each sound that you hear you are going deeper and deeper in drowsy relaxation. Number seven every muscle and every nerve is growing loose and limp and lazy. Number six you're moving down to a new and deeper level of hypnotic relaxation. Number five you are halfway down now. When I reach the count of one, I will say the words *sleep deeply*, you'll then be aware that you are more deeply relaxed than ever before. Number four each muscle and nerve lets loose, relaxing you're drifting down deeper and deeper, deeper in sleep. Number three going down deeper in drowsy relaxation. Number two — on the next number now I will give the signal. I'll say the words *sleep deeply*. When I do, you'll then be aware that you are enjoying very profound state of hypnotic relaxation. Number one sleep deeply.

Now relax and go deeper into sleep. As you go deeper into relaxation, you realize that you are a constantly growing and maturing person. You are becoming aware of the strengths and abilities that have developed within you. You feel a sense of confidence in your ability to achieve the goals you have chosen for yourself. You are learning to believe in yourself. You appreciate yourself. You do good and kind things for yourself. You meet each situation as it comes with calm and quiet assurance. You are making contact with the center of wisdom and power within you, which knows what to do and how to do it. Whatever you say, whatever you do is said and done with complete confidence and self assurance. You walk with a spring in your step. Your head is held high. You see the beauty of life around you. People respect you because you respect them and you respect yourself. You have confidence in your own judgement and you are honest and dependable. You move forward from one positive achievement to another.

You're aware that it is possible for a person to concentrate so strongly when reading, studying or working that they become completely unaware of things that happen around them. It is possible for you to concentrate like that from now on. Whenever you wish to concentrate, first get ready for the work that you are going to do. Get your books, your writing materials, the tools with which you are going to work; have them ready for the job to be done. Next look at the clock and decide how long you wish to concentrate and then write the time that you are going to end your concentration on a piece of paper. Write it three times. For example if you are beginning at seven o'clock in the evening and you decide to study until eleven o'clock in the evening. Write it three times on a piece of paper. Look at it, say it aloud three times. As you say those words, begin to concentrate. Your thoughts start to narrow to the job at hand. Your ears start to become less sensitive to surrounding noises; your eyes are drawn to the work you are about to do. Start working, if the project is reading, start reading, if it is writing, start writing. Whatever the job is, start doing it.

Within the next few minutes your concentration increases until you are oblivious to your surroundings; In the next few minutes the rest of the world seems to fade away so that for you, there exists only the job at hand and you are doing that job. Your concentration rapidly becomes perfect and remains that way until the time that you have stated arrives. Your concentration is continuous, unless there is some real and necessary reason to attend to other things. Your concentration is continuous and perfect from a few minutes after you start working until the time you have set for yourself.

Your thoughts are all directed at the job at hand. The outside world is far away. Your concentration is perfect until the time you have set for yourself. The knowledge that you acquire in this concentrated way remains in your conscious memory much longer as you read, study or work in this manner. You find your ability to remember facts, details, principles and theories is tremendously increased. You retain a perfect conscious memory of the material that you acquire in this way. You are also simultaneously developing a new ability to remember things that you had previously forgotten. You are becoming aware of a feeling of personal confidence in your intelligence.

You have confidence in your ability to master your studies. When you read, you read with an absolute concentration, and you easily remember what you read. When you listen, you listen intently, and you remember what your hear. You are confident because you have the ability to do the work, the ability to pay close attention to what is said, the ability to concentrate when you are reading, and the ability to remember what you have heard and read. While you are reviewing, your concentration on your books and notes is absolute. When reading for review it is necessary to read only once. This reading will bring to the upper levels of your mind the studies that you have already mastered. During this time you read rapidly and accurately with full understanding. When you go to the examination you are confident of your ability to write a perfect paper. You know the subject and you know that you know the subject. You are calm and self possessed. As you read the first question, a feeling will begin to develop. That feeling will be that you can easily answer the question correctly or that you are uncertain. After reading the question, if you feel the least bit uncertain, pass that question and go on to the next one. Repeat the process.

You have the knowledge to answer all of the questions correctly. As you read each question you are sending an order down to your subconscious mind. This order is that the direct answer be delivered up to the conscious level, and sometimes this takes a little while. As you are reading the next question, the answer to the first one will be working up to the memory level at the same time that you are sending down orders to the other questions. By the time you have finished reading all the questions you will be fully ready to answer the first one that you missed. Remember, if for any reason the answer seems to be a little slow in being delivered, pass that question and go on to the next one. Your second reading of the question will reinforce the order, and by the time you have finished all of the answers that come easily, the answers to the other questions will be ready for you. Remember that usually the last question counts as much as the first one. Never wait for the answer to a question until you have answered the ones that come easily to you. If the examination is an essay type, the same rule applies. Begin writing, and if you run dry or if you feel uncertain, don't waste time, move to the next question and begin writing. The second time you are back to where you left off, the answer will flow much more easily. Anytime you experience an anxious feeling, simply take a deep breath and as you exhale say mentally the words "calm," "poised," "easy recall." You are calm and poised throughout the entire examination because you are calm and confident. You work with the highest efficiency and you do it easily. When the examination is over, you are confident that you have scored the grade that you want.

Your powers of observation and awareness are improving greatly with each passing day. All that you read, hear and feel is fully detected, integrated and stored in associated patterns in your memory. You possess the key to unlock the stored memory patterns, and whatever you wish to recall flows instantly into your conscious awareness. You know that your concentration and retention are constantly improving. Your quest for knowledge keeps you mentally alert and searching. Each day you are thrilled and delighted by the rich, abundant variety of ideas and exciting philosophies that come before you. The intensely creative part of you is enriched and strengthened with each new insight. Whenever you need to remember, you send an order to your subconscious mind, an order to deliver the full and correct memory, and the idea appears with perfect clarity and form. Each time you use your memory to its full capacity you feel a deep, satisfying, inner warmth that comes from pride in yourself and your continuing success. You feel great confidence in the phrasing and organization of your ideas. You are exact and to the point. This rich confidence in your skillful use of your learning powers causes your concentration to become better, more effective, more permanent with each passing day.

Your subconscious mind is a well-spring of abundant, creative information. It contains all of the answers that are needed, and it instantly responds when needed in a calm, clear and easy way. For you, learning is a pleasurable experience. Your desire to learn is a powerful driving force that constantly motivates you towards the realization of your full potential for intellectual growth. The full understanding of what you learn comes easily, completely, and in an organized way. As your stored knowledge increases, your confidence grows by leaps and bounds. You speak with assurance on subjects you have studied, knowing you can command your subconscious mind to send forth this knowledge whenever you want it.

Because of this awareness your whole being radiates an inner glow as you work or play, revealing you as a witty, informed and expressive personality. You concentrate with an intense single mindedness, much as a river flows from its source to its mouth. Like a river, your mind flows from its source to its mouth. Like a river, your mind flows in one direction seeking out ideas and answers to the problem. As your mind flows, it grows as a river grows, with many streams flowing into it. Becoming vibrant, always seeking, searching, probing. Whenever you focus your concentration, whether upon a worn textbook or the daily newspaper you are cheerfully energetic, relaxed and poised. Printed words cause you to integrate your experiences with the ideas presented. You understand ideas the first time you encounter them. You are now reading more material rapidly and easily. Images form clearly and precisely. The relationship of ideas and concepts become clear and open as you absorb new material. As you quickly read a text you automatically find the main ideas and you instantly create a mental outline. Because you are constantly aware of the purpose of your studies and because you hold the vision of your goal constantly before you, you have continual success in your learning experiences.

Your subconscious mind is a perfect memory core. It is the sum total of all that you have studied and all that you have experienced. You are thrilled and delighted by the meaning and significance of your easy access to your subconscious memory. You continually grow in your capacity to absorb and use good information. You filter out and reject whatever is not needed. People respond to you because of your extraordinary recall, retention, your scope of interest and your depth of knowledge. This pleasant experience constantly and continually repeats itself. You are thrilled to have such a sharp and well organized memory. Now each of these ideas are making a vivid, deep, permanent impression on your subconscious mind. Not just because I have spoken to you, but because of your intense desire to incorporate these ideas into your subconscious mind. You recognize the foundation of truth from which these ideas emerge. You are becoming free of any and all beliefs you may have held in the past about your capacity for using your mental powers. Each repetition of the ideas opens up new levels of awareness for you, stimulates new insights about your true potential for the creative use of your perfect memory.

Now I am going to count from one to five. At the count of five, let your eyelids open, and you are calm, rested, refreshed, relaxed, fully aware and feeling good in every way. One: slowly, calmly, easily, gently return to your full awareness once again. Two: each muscle and nerve in your body is loose and limp and relaxed and you feel wonderfully good. Three: from head to toe you're feeling perfect in every way, mentally perfect, emotionally calm and serene. Number four: your eyes begin to feel sparkling clear, just as though they were bathed in cold spring water. On the next number now, eyelids open and fully aware and feeling good. Number five: eyelids open, now take a deep breath and fill up your lungs and stretch.

"This particular guided imagery journey I use with student or clients who find their memory is not what they would like it to be. Prior to the induction, I acquaint them with some sensible hints on how not to forget things. Some examples would be writing things down, marking the calendar for important events, using association and repeating names or whatever your trying to remember to yourself more than once. I then reinforce this with hypnosis using the above guided imagery journey."

— *Richard J. Palmer*

45

Flying Free

Guide: Victoria Bentley

The Journey

Find a comfortable place to sit or lie down and loosen any tight clothing. Take a long slow deep breath. Breathe in, inflate your abdomen, and hold it for a moment. Hold the tension and then exhale, and with the exhalation, let all the tension leave your body, leaving your muscles light and relaxed.

Focus your attention on your feet. Tense your feet, arches, and toes just enough to feel the tension. Hold the tension, but not so much to cramp your feet. Just notice the tension and then let them relax. Let your toes and feet relax.

Now focus on your calves. Tense just your calf muscles by bringing your toes upward. Feel the tension in the back of your calves. Hold the tension, notice how it feels, and then let it go.

Now tense your thigh muscles, just your thigh muscles. Feel the tension in your thighs, hold it for a moment and then let it go. Let your thigh muscles, calves and feet relax so that your legs are light and relaxed.

Now tense your buttocks and your pelvis. Tense those muscles, feeling the tightness. Hold the tightness, then let it go, so that your buttocks and pelvis relax just as your legs have.

Now focus your attention on your stomach muscles. Pull your stomach muscles in. Hold the tension, hold the tightness. Notice how your stomach feels when it is tight and then let it relax. Just let the muscles release so that the whole lower half of your body is light and relaxed.

Now take another deep abdominal breath. Slowly, fill your belly so it moves outward, letting the air continue up to fill your middle ribs and into your chest. Hold it until your chest is open and stretched, feeling the tension, and then exhale slowly, first from your abdominal, then from your middle ribs. Allow your breath to flow easily and naturally as the relaxation continues to spread through your body, leaving your muscles light and relaxed.

Now pull your shoulders toward each other, as if the front of your shoulders could touch. Feel the stretch across your back and feel the tension in your back, shoulders and neck. Hold the tension; notice how it feels and then just let your shoulders relax. Let the tension drain out of your back, like sand leaving your body. Push your shoulders up to your ears. Push them up, squeezing your neck muscles, creating pressure and tension in your neck, really push hard here. Notice how the tension feels. Hold it, then drop your shoulders like a rag doll, letting all of the tension go. All of the tension is leaving your body and draining out of your body like sand, leaving your muscles light and relaxed, leaving your mind light and relaxed.

Now focus on your jaw. Wiggle your jaw around to loosen it up, then jut your jaw way out. Jut it way out, noticing the tension in your jaw. Hold it for a moment and then let it go. Let your jaw fall slack. Release your jaw. Release the tension, so that your jaw is light and relaxed.

Now squeeze your face up like a raisin. Just squeeze it up tight, pinching your lips, nose, cheeks and eyes. Noticing how your face feels when it is tight. Hold the tension a bit longer and let it relax. Let your face soften and relax, so that your mouth and cheeks and nose and lips are all soft and relaxed. Now push your eyebrows way up. Wrinkle your brow, creating tension in your scalp, down the back of your head to your ears and the back of your neck. Then let the tension go so that your whole head, face, neck and shoulders are completely and deeply relaxed.

Now focus your attention on your biceps. Tense your biceps, just your biceps. Noticing the tension, hold it, then let it go. Now focus on your forearms. Bring your hands up like flippers. Noticing the tension in your forearms, hold it, then let them relax. Let your forearms go.

Last of all wiggle your hands to release the tension. Wiggle them once more. Make your hands into a claw for a moment and let them relax. Let your hands drop to your sides and relax so that your whole body is completely and deeply relaxed. Let go of any remaining tension you might have.

Now while your in this state of deep relaxation, imagine yourself the day before your flight, choosing what clothes you want to wear, taking time and care to pack your bags. Imagine yourself doing this cheerfully, easily thinking about the excitement of your upcoming trip.

Pause

Now imagine yourself the night before your flight. Imagine yourself sleeping like a baby completely and deeply relaxed. The next morning waking up ready to go, rested and comfortable.

Pause

Now imagine yourself driving to the airport. Notice whether you drive your own car or if you have a ride, whether you're alone or with a companion. Visualize yourself going to the airport. Trace the route that you are going to take. See yourself parking the car or getting off the air porter and walking into the terminal with your bags and your ticket. You are not in a hurry. You are comfortable and centered, as you calmly check in at the desk, making sure that your seat assignment is correct. At this time you may want to tell the flight attendant or check-in personnel that you would like to board earlier or later. You may want to explain to them that you have not been comfortable when flying in the past. Just to let them know, so that you feel you have some control over the situation; so that people there know you and care about you. You may also ask to meet the captain. You may want to shake his hand, to see his smile, to see that there is a real person flying the plane, a person that you know and trust. See yourself sitting down, waiting, breathing slowly, using the waiting period as a time to breath. Do slow abdominal breathing, calming yourself, as you look forward to the trip. Imagine what you will do when you get there. As you walk toward the ramp, down into the plane, breathing, feeling relaxed and in control. As you board, you may meet the captain. Often the captain of the airplane will show you the cockpit, or introduce you to the first officer.

Pause

Get a sense of being on the plane with other people. Know that all of you are going there together. Find your seat, sit down. Buckle in, perhaps say hello to your seat mate and begin a conversation.

Pause

Continue to breath slowly and deeply allowing your breath to flow easily and naturally. Listen to the sound of the engine; it may remind you of a cat purring , or the whirl of a blender. The door shutting will be your cue to continue to breathe slowly, abdominally, easily. See yourself enjoying being on the plane, feeling comfortable. Then with take off, imagine yourself being lifted, being supported. Imagine the plane lifting like a bird, the lightness of the plane, cradled in the arms of angels. As the plane lifts off easily, the ground softly moves into the gentleness of the clouds. You see yourself being carried aloft in a relaxed, peaceful state.

Pause

As you continue your flight, you may imagine that the plane begins to grow long legs with huge duck feet that touch across the water and land, carrying you safely to your destination. As you continue to breath deeply and easily, you are served something to drink and a meal perhaps. You may take this time to read, do a crossword puzzle, relax, be alone with your thoughts, to prepare for a presentation, or to catch up on your reading.

Pause

Before you know it, you are ready to land and again you imagine the plane cradled in the arms of angels, dropping easily and gently toward the airport with wheels down, gliding effortlessly down, touching. The bounce of the wheels, reminds you of the excitement of your destination. As the plane nestles up to its home, the tube is attached again. You leave the plane feeling light and relaxed, feeling the excitement of accomplishment, the exhiliaration of success.

"I use this guided imagery for people who have a fear of flying or who have anxiety symptoms in airplanes and avoid flying because of them."   — *Victoria Johnson*

46

Inner Golf

Guide: Doss Knighten, M.S.

The Journey

Close your eyes and when you are ready, imagine you are able to see a golf course, with green grass and trees lining the course in each of the fairways. Now imagine that you are playing the game of golf, and you want to focus your concentration in such a way that you have no distractions from the easy comfortable, powerful stroke that you hope to make — swinging the club and having the ball flying in the direction that you wish.

Now imagine your feet positioned firmly on the ground. You now grip the club firmly. The head of the club rests behind the golf ball. At this point you breath very deeply. Look down the fairway and imagine a line that the ball will make through the air, much as a tracer would make coming out the end of a gun barrel. You can see the bright line that the ball will make as it flies through the air. Now as you look back to the ball, you focus all of your attention on the club and the ball. Hold your head steady as you begin the back swing. As you bring your back swing up to its highest point, cocking your wrist, you feel very, very relaxed. Watch the ball closely, and begin the down swing with your club, watching the ball. As the club head swings on its downward arch, your body moves into the stroke. Your hips and shoulders move through. You feel the club head strike the ball and your club swings up with the follow through. You have completed the swing, and you look down the fairway and see the ball landing in the distance right in line with the line you visualized.

Now let us start again. Repeat the same process. Position the ball, look down the fairway and create the line. Look back at the ball, begin your back swing. Cock your wrist. Now begin the down swing, striking the ball with the follow through. It becomes very easy for you to pay no attention to and lose awareness of anyone standing nearby. Your total focus is on striking the ball.

Pause

Change the scene and move to the green. You now have your ball laying on the green. You take your putter in your hands. Position your feet firmly on the ground. Address the ball with your putter. As you look from the ball to the hole, you will again see a bright line. Look back at your putter again, take a deep breath, relax and begin your back swing, focusing on the ball. You start your down swing with a nice, easy, comfortable stroke and an easy follow through. The ball rolls down the line toward the hole and drops into the cup.

Pause

Again, imagine you have the ball sitting on the green and are to repeat the process. Observe the bright line from the ball to the hole. Position your feet firmly on the ground. Start your back swing. Allow yourself to strike the ball with a very easy stroke and watch the ball proceed towards the hole. Repeating this experience, practicing it, and visualizing it with each shot will allow you to have a greater and greater sense of control of your concentration and to minimize any distractions that might interfere.

"This imaging provides rehearsal of the behavior through images rather than through the physical performance of the behavior. It has been my experience, personally and with my clients, that we find significant improvement in performance by practicing successful images." — Doss Knighten, M.S.

47

Turning Insight Into Action[8]

Guide: Martin L. Rossman, M.D.

The Journey

Take a comfortable position, and have writing materials at hand. During this exercise you will often have your eyes open and will be writing. There is no need to do deep relaxation until you reach the stage of mental rehearsal.

The process of grounding is something you may or may not do well instinctively. The following process breaks it down into steps that allow you to make change happen from your insights.

The first step is to *clarify your insight*. Take some time to state to yourself as clearly and simply as you can what you have learned that you wish to act on. Write down the clearest sentence you can that expresses that insight. Carefully look at the sentence you have written and decide which word is the most important one in that sentence. Look at each word carefully and make sure that it is just the right word to express exactly what you mean. Take as much time as you need to do this.

Pause

Next, *think about your insight* and list several possible ways you might practically act on that insight to make the changes you desire. Brainstorm this—take a large sheet of paper and write down as many ways as you can think of that would be a step in this direction. Do not edit as you write. List all possibilities that come to mind, whether realistic or not.

Pause

Look over your options—can you combine any? Which would be the most practical for you to actually carry out? Which would be the simplest? The easiest? Is there one way which promises the most success or the greatest return for the least effort?

When you are ready, *choose* the option that seems the most realistic and promising for you. Circle that choice on your list.

Pause

The next step is to *affirm* your choice... to put your energy and resolve behind it. It often helps to state your choice aloud. Repeat to yourself several times "I choose to... " whatever it is you have decided to do.... Make you affirmation aloud.

Pause

The fifth step is to *make a concrete plan* for carrying out your choice. Consider what specific steps are involved and in what order.... Who might you have to speak to, and what might you have to do?... Make a specific plan in simple, yet detailed steps.... Write it down, making sure it is clear and practical.

Pause

Now *rehearse your plan in your imagination*.... Close your eyes and take a couple of deep breaths... and invite your body to relax as it has so many times before. Just allow it to be at ease and comfortable where you are. As you breathe gently and easily, allow your mind to become quiet and still.... You may want to go to your quiet inner place and become comfortable there.... When you are ready, imagine yourself actually carrying out your plan.... Really use your imagination to see and feel yourself carrying out your plan from start to finish to give yourself a sense of what may happen in real life.... Notice which parts seem easy and which parts are harder.... During your imagery you may become aware of obstacles to carrying out your plan.... These may be events, people, or simply feelings and attitudes that arise as you begin to act on your plan.... If you do envision such obstacles, adjust your plan to account for them.... You may find you need to change your plan or break it down into smaller steps to make it happen.... Take all the time you need to adjust your plan until you can imagine yourself carrying it out successfully.

Pause

Repeat your imagery rehearsal, imagining yourself successfully carrying out your plan several times, until you feel comfortable with it.... This will help you energize and support this new way of acting and reacting for you.

When you are fully ready, open your eyes and become wide-awake.... Take some time to write about any changes or adjustments you've made in your plan... and about any obstacles you have anticipated and how you might deal with them if they arise.

The final step in grounding is to *act* on your plan. Carry it out in real life for a certain amount of time.... As you do this, continue to be observant of your thoughts and feelings and notice how others react to you as you act in this new way. Notice where you are successful and where you enjoy this new way... and also notice where you have difficulty, if you do.... Do any problems you didn't anticipate arise as you act on this plan?... If so, how might you adjust to account for them?... Life is a continuous process of adjustment and refinement... pay attention, and you can learn to make change happen in the easiest and most effective way.

"I have a favorite cartoon that features a little character who's saying "My problem is, I can never separate my insight from my baloney!" That's what this script is about; separating insight from baloney." — *Martin L. Rossman, M.D.*

48

Leap

Guide: Brian L. Weatherly

The Journey

Sink your awareness down into your center. You're totally relaxed and calm.

Your skin becomes a medium of tactile awareness that enables you to feel yourself and the medium that's external to you. You're in a very fluid environment. You become aware of visual images. These images tell you that you are in a very beautiful, calm and serene surrounding. You are surrounded by a beautiful, transparent, yet slightly greenish hued medium that you feel on your skin; then you realize that you are in water.

Your eyes are very sensitive and you see ahead of you beautiful, rounded shapes — long, flowing, plant like objects. You realize suddenly that you are capable of unlimited movement in this medium, and you experience a warm and energetic flow by your skin as you move through this medium. The slightest thought of movement produces in your body that movement through the medium.

Suddenly you are aware that you are swimming through this medium with the smallest of effort. Just the thought of moving up takes you upward. Just the thought of moving down takes you downward. All of the objects that surround you are very round, very smooth and very pleasant to your eyes and to your skin. And as you brush by them you are aware that they transmit to you very smooth and sensual images. As you move upward through this medium you are aware that above you is a bright and golden light. This light seems to contain a great deal of energy. You move upward toward it.

When you are in proximity of this golden light, you suddenly realize that there is something between you and it: a barrier. A barrier that you cannot as yet break through. You hover very near this barrier because the light that comes through it is very pleasant to your skin and very pleasant to your eyes; it seems to contain a great deal of energy which you desire. You move forward and suddenly you are aware that ahead of you is a wall. A wall, an obstacle that you cannot see over because it goes up through the barrier that you find yourself hovering just underneath.

You know that you must go forward, that you must go over this barrier. You allow yourself, through relaxation, to be swept back farther from the barrier. When you can see it from a distance, you realize that this golden flow that's coming over the wall and through the barrier is where you must go. Now, with a giant leap of your imagination and a giant push of your body, you speed forward toward the flow and you propel yourself up into and through the barrier.

You are aware that all is light and brilliance around you. You realize that your body is transformed. As you leap through the barrier, your whole body transforms and becomes not of the fluid medium, but of the above the barrier, an air dweller. Look down with new eyes and see that you are now above the fluid medium that you existed in before and you see upon its surface your reflection.

Pause

You have succeeded in leaping up and over the barrier and out of the fluid medium where you were previously. Now, with the same power of mind that enabled you to move in the fluid medium you find that now you can move in the air. That the brilliant, yellow material that you found yourself so attracted to before, is all around. It is the light that fills the air. You see about you new shapes and new substances. You are aware that you now are able to move yourself with just the power of your mind. You move about freely and easily in any direction, and you are filled with the joy of your new shape and your new existence. You have succeeded in leaping over the dragon's gate.

Pause

It is time to come back to the present. Be aware of your fluid environment. As in the beginning of this journey, again feel your skin and the medium that is external to you. Bring your awareness up from center and open your eyes.

"I use this journey to help change the negative consciousness that I sometimes find myself in. When I am mired in a problem, and I realize a change of consciousness is required I examine and approach it in an entirely different way to succeed in solving it. Change is the thing that must always be kept in mind, change is the only constant." — *Brian L. Weatherly*

49

Ox Herding

Guide: Brian L. Weatherly

The Journey

Relax. Take three deep breaths and let them out slowly. Close your eyes, let yourself drift, empty your mind of all thought. You are going to a place that is far away, a long time ago.

You are a young child who lives in a clearing next to a gigantic jungle and in that jungle there are many wild and interesting things. Everyday you go into the jungle to play and discover the creatures who live there. Today as you cavort about the jungle, you see a beautiful and mysterious beast, but you only catch a glimpse of him in the distance, through the dark jungle. Try as you may, you cannot again find this beast, this wonderous beast. The next day again, you catch just a glimpse of this beautiful, gigantic beast and you recognize that it is a large ox with beautiful, big horns and a sleek, fine coat. All you see is a small glimpse of the beast. The next day, however, you see the beast clearly. You try to go near him, but he quickly runs away and hides in his jungle haunts and you return sadly to your village. The next day you enter the jungle, and as if he were waiting for you,

you see him almost at once. You are amazed when he allows you to approach, but not too close. As you come closer, the ox snorts, and again, returns to his jungle haunts quickly. Sadly, you return to your village that night. The next day, as you go forth into the jungle, the ox appears almost immediately. The ox allows you to approach very near, and indeed, even to touch his hide, his shiny coat. You are filled with joy as the powerful ox allows you to stroke his side and spend some time together.

Pause

That night, you wish the ox to return to your village but no, the ox once more disappears into the jungle. The next day you enter the jungle and almost immediately find the ox. This time you come prepared with a small halter to hopefully capture the ox. You are surprised, even amazed, when the ox allows you to place the halter about his snout and lead him a little way here and there, however, the ox is not easily tamed and soon wants to return to his jungle haunts. You persevere, however, and each time the ox tries to go about his wild ways, you tug at the halter and gently persuade the ox to come back and go in the direction that you want. Soon, through constant, gentle urging, you have succeeded in taming the ox to such an extent that he will allow himself to be led here and there, although still, he wants to return to his old ways, and it is often difficult to bring him to your bidding. Soon however, with constant perseverance you are able to direct the giant, powerful ox, and indeed he goes almost without your urging in the direction you wish him to go. Soon, the ox and you are as one, and you have only to think of the direction that you wish him to go and he complies, docile and obedient. At this point, the ox disappears and you realize that the ox himself, and all, are part of the void, the essence of the universe and us.

Your mind is much like that of the wild ox. At first, it is very difficult to capture and bring under control, but with perseverance and constant practice, your mind, like a giant beast, can slowly be brought under dominion. Once control has been established, your mind will perform at your bidding. Then the mind itself is forgotten. Once the mind is brought under control and quieted, then real understanding will dawn upon you. With that understanding everything seems easier.

Now take three deep breaths and let them out slowly. When you are ready open your eyes.

"Ox Herding is an analogy for the control of the mind. This is an ancient Buddhist analogy. The ox represents the mind. You represent the person who wishes to control your mind and behavior." — *Brian L. Weatherly*

50

Skill Rehearsal/
Master Teacher[9]
Guide: Maureen Murdock

The Journey

Stand with your weight evenly balanced over your feet and take a deep breath. In your mind's eye, see yourself involved in the skill you have chosen to improve. Now practice it for a minute with your physical body, as well as you can in the space in which you are standing.

Pause

Now practice it for a minute with your kinesthetic body.

Pause

Now sit down in a comfortable position and close your eyes. Focus your attention on your breath, following your breath in… and out… of your nostrils. As you continue to breathe, you find yourself becoming more relaxed.

Now imagine that you are out hiking and you find yourself on a path in a very thick forest. The forest appears to be very friendly, so you continue down a path until you come to a group of very tall trees. As you approach this group of trees, you notice that one of the trees has a door in it. You open the door and walk into a small hallway. The hallway leads you down a stone staircase. You begin to go down the stairs, down... down... down. Finally you come to a great room that is filled with wonderful inventions that you have never seen before. You walk around the room, amazed by all that you see. You follow another corridor until you find yourself in a room that feels very peaceful and familiar. There you meet the Master Teacher of your skill, someone who can teach you all you want to know. This Teacher may speak to you in words or in actions; either will be very effective for you. You have three minutes of clock time equal to all of the time that you need to learn from your Master Teacher.

Pause

Now you will leave your Master Teacher, thanking this person and knowing that you can return any time you wish. Walk back through the corridor, through the room of the marvelous inventions, up the staircase, and out through the door in the tree. You close the door and walk back through the forest. And then you find yourself sitting here. When you are ready, open your eyes, stand up, and rehearse your skill with your physical body.

Pause

Stop. Rehearse your skill with your kinesthetic body.

Pause

Now again with your physical body.

Pause

Now this time, as you do it again with your kinesthetic body, notice if there is more for you to learn about your skill. Is there a new approach that you can try? If so, try this with your kinesthetic body and then again physically. Notice any improvement that you have made, and notice too, how you feel about your ability.

"In this exercise we use the image of a "Master Teacher" to help improve a specific skill. Begin by choosing a skill that you wish to improve or perfect. It may be soccer, writing, painting or whatever it is that you wish to improve." — *Maureen Murdock*

51

Smoker–Non-Smoker

Guide: Jessie Greene, L.M.S.W.

The Journey

Just begin to imagine yourself sitting comfortably in your chair. Experience yourself letting go of any tension in your body. Begin to feel more and more relaxed as you sink deeper and deeper into your chair as you just give yourself permission to become calmer, more serene, and more relaxed with every breath. Take a deep breath, breathing in relaxation while you exhale any tension. As you proceed with this exercise and thoughts come into your mind, just see them enter one side, and go right out the other. This is time you have taken to be good to yourself, to feel good about who you are becoming, to feel good about what you are about to experience.

You now find yourself walking down a long hall. With every step you find yourself going deeper and deeper into your subconscious. At the end of the hall you become aware of the presence of two doors. Over one door is a sign that says "Smokers" and over the other door the sign says "Non-Smokers." You hesitate for a moment, this is your chance, your chance at a new beginning. But can you do it? What might you be passing up? Perhaps there is something yet to experience behind that door marked "Smokers." Then you begin to remember... the clothes you have burnt, the dirty ashtrays, your health, the look on the faces of people you care about. And yet, there are other memories. Times shared with cigarettes. What will these experiences look like now, without cigarettes. Who are you without your cigarettes? You have tried this before. Are you ready for another failure? What can make this time different? *"I am a non-smoker."* How does that sound? *"I am a non-smoker!"* That time it was said easier. "I AM A NON-SMOKER." You reach for the door marked "Non-Smoker." O.K., let's go for it.

As you open the door you begin to hear a crowd roaring. Hey, it's you they have been waiting for. These are all the people who have gone before you. The ones who have stopped smoking. The ones who did it. The ones who decided no longer to sit and ponder "Will I or won't I." The numbers of these people are enormous. They are all in your corner. They are aware of your struggle and they are with you. They know you CAN do it. There goes another roaring cheer... for you! The crowd is with you. As they part aside, you see in front of you, a gondola. You climb into the gondola. Weighing the gondola down are stale tobacco odors and packs of cigarettes. You pick up a pair of magic scissors. You are told they are magic because they can cut you free from that by which you no longer wish to be tied and weighted down. You begin to cut the ropes. With each snip, the scissors cut easier and more assured. As you cut the last rope, you begin to rise, easily and effortlessly into the air. The air seems so light, so pure, so life-giving. You are feeling so good about what you are doing. As you rise higher and higher, into the air, you again hear the fading roar of the crowd, your cheering squad.

You now realize that you have begun a new course. As you begin to travel, you look out of the gondola and see yourself below, doing things that you have been unable or unwilling to do for so long. You are able to engage in physical activities, no longer hampered. You are able to sit anywhere you want, with anyone you want. Your choices are broadening. Your thoughts are clearer, your clothes cleaner. You have more money to spend and enjoy. You no longer notice people moving away from you. You feel very proud of yourself. It wasn't easy, but you did it, and you were not alone. Anytime you feel weak, you will remember the roar of the crowd, the lightness of the gondola, the experience of soaring high above, and you will remember how you now look, as a non-smoker... confident, serene, determined. Take a moment and look at yourself. As you finish this experience, tuck all these memories away. They will be there anytime you need them. This is an experience that is now a part of who you are, as you again find yourself sitting back on your chair, in the room, at this time, having made a decision for a new beginning.

"It is very important for smokers to begin to visualize themselves as non-smokers and to verbally state such." — *Jessie Greene*

52

Weigh/In-Weigh/Off®

Guide: Norton Wyner, Ph.D.

The Journey

As your breathing slows into relaxed regularity, your imagination may prepare for the start of this wonderful trip of change. The rhythm of your breathing merges into all of the regular rhythms of the universe. The rhythm of time and tides. The rhythm of our planet orbiting in space.

The rhythm of a lonely, huge, irregularly shaped boulder balanced at the top of a mountain. The solitary boulder rocks a bit, side to side... side to side and then almost imperceptibly, forward and back as you stand behind it.... Gently, forward and back, as though it chooses to come down from its lonely perch... all the way down to the level valley at the bottom of the mountain... where it doesn't have to stay perched at the pinnacle. And so, quite slowly the boulder begins to ease down from its perch. Ever so slowly.

And as it meanders down the mountain, brushing up against one obstacle after another, we see that the boulder isn't quite solid. All sorts of matter are left behind here and there. So what seemed solid rock was many rocks and debris held together. Halfway down the mountain, the boulder has shed half of its original size, and as it comes to rest, finally, at the bottom, it's been transformed to only its very inner core... a smooth and attractive gemstone. It glistens in the sun — freed of the years of collected debris.

It rolls to rest, joining other shining gemstones. Oh yes, each is quite individual in size and color. All proudly reflect back the healing rays of the sun. They rest there... relieved, happy and content.

Happy, content, giving off the radiance of your new inner peace and tranquility. Just as your heart will pulsate with joy, love and happiness as you shed the accumulated debris of overweight.

Just as you will shed your weight on the voyage from your loneliness down to join the beauty of proper weight.

And each obstacle on your voyage will become a triumph as you leave behind the unwanted... and as the lighter you glows with empowerment and control and the certainty of success.

"Our WEIGH/IN-WEIGH/OFF® program starts with immediate imaging of a logic-based success metaphor. Subsequent sessions begin with affirmation of this metaphor. Patients are urged to start their day with this guided image, adding it to their plan for the day... to be assessed at bedtime, with a repeat of the guided image. Care must be taken to assure that patient has no problem with heights or falling." — Norton Wyner, Ph.D.

Freedom and Awareness

53

Exploring the Rim

Guide: Mary Margaret Miller, MSW

The Journey

To begin, seat yourself in a comfortable position, uncross your arms and legs and be aware of your breathing. Just observe it and feel it. Take three slow deep breaths. With the inhale, scan your body. Scan for areas that may be tight or knotted. With the exhale, breathe into those areas. Start at your feet and breathe in and scan, and exhale and release.

Pause

Finally breathe in clean, fresh and lightened breath. Release any tension, thoughts or distractions. Just breathe normally.

As you continue to breathe, create a spot in the middle of your forehead. Find yourself beginning to shrink into that spot. As you breathe, you are miniaturizing yourself into the middle of your forehead.

Pause

Now move down your body in your miniature form to your solar plexus. In that spot, is located your very special and personal hole. Begin to move toward the rim of that hole. As you continue to allow your breath to relax you and keep you safe, walk towards the edge of your hole.You can notice whether it is dark or light. You can notice any colors; notice everything you see. Does the terrain change as you approach the rim of your hole.

Pause

Now notice what it feels like when you walk along this rim. Can you walk easily? Do you need to get on your hands and knees to negotiate the rim? What does it feel like?

Pause

As you continue to explore the rim, are there sounds? Of what smells are you aware?

Pause

As you feel your senses come alive on the edge of this rim and you continue to move around it, notice what thoughts come into your mind. What memories or images are evoked? What are you feeling? Beneath that feeling, what are you feeling? Beneath that feeling, what are you feeling? Beneath that feeling, what are you feeling? Breathe into and through each of your feelings.

Pause

Continue for a moment to explore the rim. Move as close to the edge as you feel comfortable, and move away sometimes and notice the shape. Let in all of the experience, all of the senses, all of the thoughts, all of the feelings, all of the wants and needs and all of your intentions.

Pause

If you come to a spot that is painful or difficult for you, stay still and breathe through it. Just notice and breathe through the feelings, breathe through the memories, breathe through the thoughts.

Pause

As you move around the rim a little more you know this is a place to which you can come to whenever you choose. You can continue to explore it. You can continue to feel safe here. It can even become a place of retreat, a haven for you. There is always the wonder, the question, the excitement about what is in the middle. What might be in the hole that your personal rim surrounds? For now thank yourself for the experience you have given yourself, and prepare to leave the rim at this time. Gradually move away from the rim, remembering that you can return here anytime you choose. As you breathe, expand yourself gradually into your body, breathe and expand yourself until you take up your entire body again. You can feel all the way to the edge of your skin. As you breathe deeply to fill your body, wiggle your fingers, wiggle your toes, move your neck, and when you are ready, open your eyes.

"Exploring the rim addresses that hole of which most of us are aware and many of us are afraid. It is a way to become more familiar, comfortable and safer with the rim of our own personal unknowings." — *Mary Margaret Miller*

54

Gypsy Moon

Guide: Lynn Roberty

The Journey

Find a quiet place to relax. Lie down on your back in a comfortable position. Place your hand on your abdomen. Feel your hand rise with each intake and fall when you exhale. Continue breathing, allowing your body to relax and become heavy against the surface on which you are lying. Feel the difference in temperature where your skin is exposed to the air and where it is covered. When you inhale feel the air flowing through your body. Feel it flowing down your arms and out of your fingers. Allow yourself to relax.

It is midnight on a warm starlit summer night. You are walking through a thick rain forest that is bathed in a beautiful silver light. The moss beneath your feet is soft and damp, cushioning your every step as you move silently through the moonlit forest. The air smells sweet and fresh, like new life. You are guided down this path by a soothing silver light. There is a clearing before you. There is an indigo pool of water. It is bathed in silver moonlight and surrounded by silver flowers that sing in the night. You now feel warm and free. Walking towards the water, you slowly begin to remove the outer covering. No longer bound by the things of this earth, your spirit is drawn to the pool. You feel strong, free, wild and lighter. You feel as if you could fly. Walk into the water. It is cool and healing. Dive deep beneath the surface allowing the water to support your body. Free the spirit. As you rise to the surface and stand in the center of the pool, a beautiful silver light from the heavens surrounds you. This light is special. This silver light is filled with hope, freedom, strength, love and peace. Stand in the light, raising your face and arms to this glorious light. Breathe deeply. Breathe in peace, and it flows through you. Breathe in strength. It fills and fortifies your soul. Breathe in freedom, and it washes away the lies that bind us. Breathe in hope, that these wondrous gifts shall stay with you. As you dance in the moon light, know this pool of magic water will always be where you can find it. The silver healing light stays within. You are free; full of peace, strength, love and hope. The Gypsy dances in silver light to silent music of the spirits. She is free now. Watch her fly.

Pause

You are becoming aware of the weight of your hand resting on your abdomen. You are again aware of the air touching your skin, your back against the surface of what you are lying on. You are becoming more aware. When you are ready, allow yourself to return to the normal state of consciousness. When you are ready you may open your eyes feeling strong, peaceful, alert and free.

"I meditate on this when I am stressed or feeling constricted. This vision re-connects me with my senses and helps me feel free and strong." — *Lynn Roberty*

Inner Child/Family

55

Inner Child

Guide: Margot Escott, M.S.W.

The Journey

When you have yourself in a comfortable, safe, relaxed position, begin focusing on your breath — in and out — like gentle waves coming in and going out. As you pay attention to your breath, let go of any thoughts or feelings that you don't need right now. Just allow yourself to drift into that pleasant state of trance where you feel comfortable and peaceful.

See yourself standing in front of an oval mirror. Reflected is a vision of yourself today. This is a special magic mirror. As you continue to gaze, you see that you are getting younger and younger. See yourself five years ago, then fifteen. See yourself getting smaller and smaller until you see an image of a very small child, perhaps three or four, five or six; whatever age feels right to you. This little child is smiling and extending his or her hand to you. As he steps out of the mirror you take hold of that small hand and begin to walk down a familiar road with that child. Feel the softness of that hand. Look at those vulnerable, trusting eyes. You may need to let that child know that you are a safe adult and are there to protect and play with that special child.

Pause

You begin to realize that the familiar road on which you are walking is the street where you lived when you were very small. You and the child approach the front door of this dwelling, perhaps a house, apartment or trailer; and, if the child needs reassurance, you let him know that the worst is over and that he is safe with you. As you walk through the front door what do you see? What rooms are you in? Who is in there? What are they doing?

Pause

You continue to walk through this place noticing the textures of the floors and walls. Noticing smells that are familiar from so long ago. You go into the kitchen. Who is in there and what are they doing? You walk to the family room and again note who is there and what they are doing. How do you feel? What does you inner child want you to know about this house and these people?

Pause

You now come into a very special room. It is the room of your precious inner child. He may have some things, special toys or objects, that he wants to share with you. Be aware of how full of life and wonder this child is. As you visit with the child, you let him know, that if he wants to, he may leave this house and come and stay with you. Let your child decide what he wants to do. If he chooses not to come today, tell him you will keep coming to visit him and he can leave with you whenever he wants. If your child decides to come, he may want to pack some things in a little bag or he may be ready to go right now. See yourself and the child walking back to the front door. As you start to leave the house, you see Mom and Dad standing in the doorway, waving and smiling good-bye. They seem happy to see you starting an exciting journey. You walk from the house, look over your shoulder and see them continuing to wave. You walk down that old familiar street and each time you turn around Mom and Dad are still there, getting smaller and smaller. You finally turn a corner, and they are no longer in sight. You find yourself in a beautiful place in nature and sit and hold that precious child in your arms. You may want to give that precious child some affirming messages like, "I am so glad that you are here; I will always love you; or You are enough." Be open to whatever that child has to tell you.

Pause

As you continue to hold the child, he becomes smaller and smaller and smaller until he is so small that you could hold him in the palm of your hand. You gently place your magical inner child in your heart, and when you look down you see the eyes looking up at you and you realize that, from now on, wherever you are, wherever you go, you are carrying the precious cargo of that special child. Let yourself be giving to that child and attend to his needs. Let the spirit of that child enter into you as you behold the wonder of each new day and the blessing of each new relationship that comes into your life.

When you are ready, slowly bring yourself back to normal waking consciousness.

"This journey has been particularly freeing for adult children who are letting go of a painful past and beginning to heal relationships with parents. I play soft lullaby music to accompany this journey, such as Steve Halpern's "Lullabies".   — *Margot Escott*

56

Journey Into Childhood

Guide: Mina Sirovy, Ph.D.

The Journey

As you close your eyes, take a deep breath. Feel your body slow down. Your breathing deepens, your body settles in, the heart slows and your mind clears. Allow all thoughts to simply pass by without emotion or analysis.

You walk down stairs, one step at a time, relaxing more with each step. Let your feet sink deeply into the carpeting on the stairs as you count twenty steps, going deeper and deeper into relaxation. When you reach the bottom of the stairs you feel safe and relaxed.

Pause

Decide now to go outdoors. Walk to the door, turn a golden key and open it on to a beautiful outdoor scene. Ask yourself, as an eight-year-old, what would be fun to do on this beautiful day? What did I do at recess that I liked? In your mind's eye, walk down a grassy slope on your short eight-year-old legs and come to a lovely green park. Suddenly you have roller skates on your feet, and they propel you up and down and around on the concrete walks that swerve through the park. You are exhilarated and free!

Pause

You notice a swing set; so you remove your magic skates and sit on the swing. It's fun to see how high you can go on your own power. You pull back your legs on each back swing and launch out farther. Soon you're flying, looking up at the beautiful blue sky, the thin, pale crescent moon, and a few wispy clouds. The wind is blowing its mellow breath on your face, hair and cheeks, and you laugh for the freedom of it all. Yes, there's a silver slide that you must try. It winds down and is fun for one way, but too structured for your newfound free self. Just at your feet there is a discarded jump rope, so you pick it up gleefully, jump a few times, then sing and dance

Pause

What a wonderful day you are having. No cares or responsibilities. There is a fountain of cool, refreshing water to soothe your throat. On impulse you stand under the high fountain and feel the water going down through your body as well as all over it. Feel it going down through your head, sinuses, throat and shoulders — relaxing as it goes, cleansing, healing, uncluttering. It's washing through your lungs, stomach, hips, thighs, knees, calves and ankles, coming out through your feet. Release all toxins in your system to the middle of the earth where they are purified in the center of molten lava. Feel the connection to the green earth. Step forward and feel the energy of the earth traveling up through your toes, ankles, legs, torso, neck and head. Feel the warmth of the energy, and see yourself inwardly and outwardly as a glowing being. Feel smaller than your body and more expanded than your body at the same time. You are a child and an adult all at once! You are not alone — you are all one. You are you and that's enough. You are here now, not a human doing but a human being.

Your body keeps breathing as you count slowly from one to ten, coming up, coming back, feeling refreshed and revived. And so it is.

"Guided Imagery is a way of controlling my mind/body through my creative unconscious, which is often tuned into cosmic consciousness." — *Mina Sirovy, Ph.D.*

57

Mother

Guide: Larry Moen

The Journey

Close your eyes. Let your mind relax and drift gently until you find yourself standing at the top of three steps. Take the first step down. Your muscles relax. Feeling heavier with each step, descend to the next level. You come to the third and final step. You step down and are totally relaxed.

You are any age you choose to be at this time. You begin to walk forward. In the distance you see a house. As you approach, it becomes clear to you that this is your mother's house. This is where your mother lives. You come closer and upon reaching the door you knock. Your mother opens the door and is standing before you. You step forward and embrace her. This hug unites you both. It represents total acceptance from both of you. She accepts you and you accept her, unconditionally. During this visit you let down all walls. You open yourself to her and let her in. You are free to express yourself knowing it is safe. You love her with all of your being, body and spirit. You both walk through the house to the kitchen. As she sits on a chair, you pull another directly in front of her. You sit down, facing her, looking deeply into her eyes. Tell her something that you have always wanted to say to her.

Pause

She is receptive to everything that you have told her. She is appreciative of your openness and your honesty, and she is proud of you. You will always be in her heart and soul. Words that you have feared for so long weren't so hard to say after all. You take her hands in your hands. You rise together, hold each other and walk back through the house to the front door. You hug each other, then the two of you separate, and you leave her standing at the door as you walk farther and farther away. You turn and wave. She waves back and the palms of your hands unite at a distance with a beam of energy and a oneness between the two of you. A oneness at a distance. The energy between your palms is strong, healthy and mature. This is the woman who has given you birth. She is a tower of strength and you are a part of her. The two of you are united in a healthy way, healthier than ever before. You place your palm to your lips and blow her a kiss that she catches in her hands and holds against her breast. Knowing you can return at any time, you find yourself at the base of three steps.

As you step up to the first step you become more awake, more energetic. You feel your body again, light and relaxed. Step up to the second step, awakening with each step you take. Gently stretch and release every muscle in your body. Now step up to the third and final step. Take a deep breath, exhale and, when you are ready, open your eyes.

"This journey gives me a certain amount of strength to express my feelings to my mother in person."   *— Larry Moen*

58

Seeking Enlightenment

Guide: James C. Kight, Jr.

The Journey

Close your eyes and visualize before you two rows of tall pine trees. Begin to feel their vibrations. Listen to the wind as it blows softly through the branches. The wind brings to you the fresh scent of pine. Draw this scent into your being. Walk from east to west between the two rows of pine trees. As you come to the other end of the path, see a swimming pool twenty feet wide and thirty-three feet long. This pool is filled with shimmering water that has a golden glow. Standing at the edge of this pool, visualize bathing in this glow for a few moments.

Pause

Now remove your outer garments. Feel the wind and the glow. Now enter the pool from the east and swim or float, slowly letting the refreshing water surround your body. Immerse your entire body in the refreshing gold water. Feel it flow through you, softly, gently, going into your pores, deep within you. Enjoy the feeling. Feel the water flow over you as you move. Enjoy this feeling as you move.

Pause

You are now on the west side of the pool. Step slowly out of the comforting and cleansing water. Two guides are there with towels to dry you. They present you with a robe (color of your choosing) and place golden sandals on your feet. When they are finished, you look up, and see a pyramid.

At the entrance door say the words, "I am one with the Christ Spirit. May I enter?" Then proceed three quarters of the way up to the top. Visualize a room with an altar made of beautiful marble. As you go to the altar to kneel. You see a window before you. Pick out a star in the heavens and say, "Guide me over the hills and valleys so that I may not stumble; let me lift my left hand up towards Thee as my right hand, I extend to help others." Remain in this position for a few moments and receive the enlightenment that comes from your guides.

Pause

Slowly relax and come out of the meditation.

"In memory of my Teacher, Cash Bateman."
— *James C. Kight, Jr.*

Creativity and Inspiration

59

Chakra Balancing/ Dreamer

Guide: Chrystle Clae

The Journey

Take a lingering deep breath, filling the bottom of your lungs first. (This means the area near your abdomen will rise filled with air before the completion of your inhale, which is when your chest rises.) Hold that breath for a mental count of six...,then exhale slowly and gently through slightly parted lips. Repeat this breath exercise several times. Make a mental note of any places in your physical body that may be holding onto the tension or pressure of your day. Breathe into those areas and feel the tensions release on your exhale.

Pause

Imagine in your mind's eye any red object — now imagine a spiral of light in that same red shade. See or feel that red spiral of energy pulsating at the base of your spine. Breathe into it and make it more vivid. Let it remain alive and vibrant as you...

Imagine in your mind's eye any orange object — now

imagine a spiral of light in that same orange shade. See or feel that orange spiral of energy pulsating in the reproductive organ area of your spine. Breath into it and make it more vivid. Let the orange remain as you...

Imagine in your mind's eye any yellow object — now imagine a spiral of light in that same yellow shade. See or feel that yellow spiral of energy pulsating in the belly-button area of your spine. Breathe into it and make it more vivid. Let the yellow remain as you...

Imagine in your mind's eye any green object — now imagine a spiral of light in that same green shade. See or feel that green spiral of energy pulsating in the area of your heart. Breathe into it and make it more vivid. Let the green light remain as you...

Imagine in your mind's eye any blue object — now imagine a spiral of light in that same blue shade. See or feel that blue spiral of energy pulsating in the throat chakra area of your spine. Breathe into it and make it more vivid. Let the blue remain as you...

Imagine in your mind's eye any deep red-blue color — now imagine a spiral of light in that same indigo shade. See or feel that indigo spiral of energy pulsating in the third eye area of your brow. Breathe into it and make it more vivid. Let the indigo remain as you...

Imagine in your mind's eye any violet object — now imagine a spiral of light in that same violet shade. See or feel that violet spiral of energy pulsating at the top, or crown, of your head. Breathe into it and make it more vivid. Let the violet remain.

Now take an imaginary step back and view your spiritual body as the beautiful rainbow that your are... a pulsating rainbow of light that is able to feel a oneness with all life in the universe. Take another slow, deep breath and find yourself in a magical summer woods. It's warm outside, so you have on a bathing suit and can feel the cool earth beneath your bare feet.

You're walking on a cleared, dirt path beneath beautiful, tall trees. You're in shade, except for the few rays of sunshine that filter in through the branches and leaves.

There are hills throughout this forest and you can see a few animals scurry about. If you look up in the trees you'll see a few birds of the forest flying from one tree to the other and occasionally touching ground...just beyond your reach.

Continue walking on your path and notice anything in the surroundings that attract you.

Pause

Now, if you look off to your right, you will see you're approaching a small cave. Go closer.

Above the opening to the cave, someone has placed the sacred symbol for Om on a woodcarving at the entrance. It's just resting on a rock. You know that this symbol is meant to assure protection and blessings to all who enter this cave.

To the left of the entrance is a smal,l natural spring flowing into a stream. The spring falls from a place just high enough so that it will act as a shower for you. On the right hand side of the cave's entrance is a clean bench where you see that someone has already placed your bed pillow and a clear quartz crystal.

Go beneath the shower of the spring and realize, as it washes you, that this is sacred and holy water that cleanses your spirit as well as your body. This is a purifying spring — allow it to remove any past spiritual hurts. It will enable you to find forgiveness for any hurts you feel you may have caused others. Let it cleanse your aura, your heart and your mind!

Pause

As you leave the spring you find that the water didn't leave you wet at all — only refreshed.

Go to the bench with your pillow and the crystal. Stop as you pick them both up and feel the Earth Mother beneath your feet once more. Close your imaginary eyes and feel the balance within your spirit as the Earth allows you to anchor your emotions and feel secure and grounded by her love.

Pause

Purified and grounded you can take your pillow and crystal and enter this special cave. Just inside its entrance, you can feel a soft breeze brush your cheek and hair. This is the breeze of Inspiration which encircles your being like a bubble. Its gift is to send you dreams of inspiration that will include symbols for your Teaching Shield. It will be with you, unseen, every time you sleep and request help or guidance from your dreams.

There is a small chamber off to the right in this cave. This is where you are to place your pillow and crystal. The chamber glows from an ultra-violet flame that has no heat. This flame will cleanse any unwanted energy from your belongings and then charge them with enhanced life and energy to be used as aids for your dream work.

The pillow will lull you to sleep and direct you to the higher vibrations of reality in the dreaming state.

The crystal given to you is charged to stimulate your connection to the universe, enabling you to have any information you need to aid you in this incarnation, through your dreams. The stone will also record your dreams for you so that remembering them after you awake will be easy.

With that charging complete, the ultra-violet flame's light reflects from your stone directly to your third eye area. This is an added blessing to stimulate your dreaming experiences.

Take a moment, as you exit this cave, to once more feel the earth beneath your feet grounding and nurturing your spirit. Glance down at the stone in your hand and see if it has remained a quartz crystal, or if the charging process in the caves chamber changed it to a different stone that better suits your vibration and needs. Any stone that remains is perfect for you.

Breathe deeply and open your eyes when you feel ready.

"I use this imagery in my workshops on Dreams and Personal Symbology. Our subconscious has all the answers to any conscious questions we may have and often shares that information in the form of dreams. This imagery aids us in remembering that powerful information and in retrieving it from our Higher Self."
— *Chrystle Clae*

60

Creative Resources

Guide: Martin Rosenman, Ph.D.

The Journey

Close your eyes and prepare to go into a deep and wonderful state of relaxation. Focus on your breath, and as you inhale and exhale say the number one to yourself each time that you exhale. Allow yourself to become more and more relaxed each time that you say the number one to yourself as you exhale.

Pause

Picture yourself in a very relaxing setting. Allow yourself to become more and more relaxed as you picture and experience your relaxing setting. Allow yourself to become more and more relaxed as you relax all parts of your body. Now feel a sensation in your right big toe. It can be a warm sensation, a relaxed sensation, a heavy sensation, a tingling sensation, a numb sensation or it can be a combination of these sensations. Let the sensation spread to your next toe, to your middle toe. Continue slowly spreading the sensation throughout the parts of your body, finishing with the parts of your head.

Pause

When your thoughts turn to the consideration of important decisions and important problems for which you have not yet found a solution, you will find that you will be able to focus and concentrate on these topics more effectively. Even when you are not consciously thinking about the problems you would like to solve, your mind will come up with many potentially useful ideas. Some of these ideas are even likely to catch you by surprise, emerging into your awareness while you are thinking of something else. They may occur during sleep when you dream, when you think of an idea in the middle of the night, or when you have ideas upon awakening. These ideas will be helpful to you, but you will always try to make sure that you have sufficient information on which to base any final decision. You will want to check out these new ideas to make sure that they are practical, just as you would check out information from any other source.

Overall, you will be pleased at how much more clearly and creatively you will be able to think.

Picture yourself doing well in a future situation. See yourself, hear yourself, experience yourself performing at the peak of your abilities. You are focused mentally and other people are responding to your positive energy. Mentally rehearse your success for your specific, future, important occurrence.

Inhale deeply, tense and relax all body parts and open your eyes when you are ready.

"This is a simple and powerful method for helping discover your creative resources. It provides a way for mentally rehearsing future events, which can lead to better performance."
— *Martin Rosenman, Ph.D.*

61

Spiral

Guide: Joseph G. Spano, M.D.

The Journey

This meditation is best done in a reclining position or supine. Have your arms up above your head, feet are apart. Let your breathing become easy and gentle, bringing the breath in from a great distance, letting it pass gently through the body and out.

Now visualize, about one or two feet above the crown of your head, radiations of brilliant, white diamond rays. Say audibly the invocation that brings forth the soul energy: "I am the soul. I am the light divine. I am love. I am will. I am fixed design."

Now see the star move down, spiraling in a clockwise way around the crown, behind the head, in front of the brow, and then to the back of the head. It then moves down the neck, front and back; past the heart, front and back; to the solar plexus, front and rear; to the lower abdomen; to the sexual energy zone, front and back; to the roots or base of the spine where it spirals down and turns, coming now to the very center of your spine. It moves past the coccyx (tail bone) to the root area, spiraling and forming a channel of brilliant, white light through the very center of the body as it travels up along the spinal cord and out the top of the head.

Pause

Repeat this process once more. Imagine the stars and the spirals around the crown, brow, throat, chest, upper abdomen, lower abdomen. See it turn and come into the lower portion of the body at the base of the spine where it spirals up through the center of the body, through the lower abdomen, solar plexus, heart, throat, middle of the brain or brow, drown, and up and out. Now see it come back through the crown, brow, throat, and into the heart. The sould star is in the heart. It pulsates white light and moves over to the spleen and the left upper abdomen, into the solar plexus, and into the heart, and into the upper chest. Then it spirals down into the lower abdomen, into the sexual energy zone, then up to the throat, down to the base of the spine and the root, then up to the thrid eye or brow. Now it sprials over to the left elbow, the left knee, the right knee, the right elbow, and the crown. The star moves to the left hand, the left foot, the right foot, the right hand, and then two or three feet above the crown in the transpersonal zone. The brilliance intensifies, and the star comes once more through the crown, past the third eye, through the throat, heart, solar plexus, and into the center of the abdomen within one to two inches of the navel. For men, it spirals thrity-six times clockwise and twenty-four time counter clockwise. For women, it spirals thrity-six times counterclockwise and twenty-four times clockwise.

Pause

Now the star moves into the sexual energy zone, just above the pubic bone. As it pulsates, it moves to the mid-abdomen, navel area, base of the spine, and the coccyx. Now it moves up the back to a spot corresponding to the navel, to a point corresponding with the solar plexus, and then to the base of the skull, into the crown, into the third eye, and by way of the tongue into the throat.

Visualize rays of silver and white light passing from the third eye by way of the tongue which, touches the pallet, on into the throat. Visualize it moving from the throat into the heart, from the heart into the solar plexus, and then again into the navel area. Now all the channels are open, and the star moves to the solar plexus and into the heart where it pulsates intensely. It fills the heart with the energy of unconditional love, a perfect love, a healing, harmonizing and heightening love. The heart fills with this energy, and it overflows into the shoulders and the arms and the hands. Place your hands over the navel area, and imagine the energy flowing from the palms into the navel area. Visualize the energy radiating from the hands into the umbilical area, several inches into the abdomen. Perhaps your vision is one of white light or a propane flame or radiations of light from the star. The energy heightens, harmonizes and heals. Move the hands over the lower abdomen, the soul star is in the heart pulsating, filling the heart with the energy of unconditional love, that nurturing healing, heightening energy. It overflows into the arms, down into the hands and radiates through the palms into the lower abdomen into all the organ structures in that area.

Now move the hands down to the very base of the spine near the anal opening and radiate the energy of love into that area. The soul star is in the heart pulsating and nurturing, sending, healing energy that overflows into the arms, down into the hands and pulsates from the palms into the very root of your being. Now lift up a bit and allow the hands to be underneath the coccyx, at the base of the spine, behind you and radiate the healing energy of love into the coccyx. The soul star is in the heart; it pulsates; it overflows into the palms and radiates loving energy into the coccyx. Now move the fingertips to an area on the back that corresponds to the navel in front. The soul star is in the heart radiating the energy of unconditional love, healing, harmony, and nurturing. It overflows from the heart into the arms and hands. The fingertips radiate this energy into the spine and body. Visualize the energy leaving the fingertips, and now move your fingertips up higher to a point that corresponds to the very bottom of the breast bone but in the back. (If necessary, use the sides of the hands both right and left.)

Now visualize the soul star in the heart pulsating, filling the heart with the energy of love as it overflows into the shoulders, arms, and hands. Radiate the energy into the solar plexus from behind. The energy harmonizes, heightens and heals. The nurturing energy allows you to release anger and resentment, hostilities, and feelings of inadequacy. And in its place, fills the whole area with perfect love. Now bring the hands forward to the very base of the skull with one palm upon the other and radiate the energy into the neck, just below the base of the skull. The soul star is in the heart pulsating, filling the heart with the energy of unconditional love. It overflows into the arms, hands, and palms as it radiates energy into the base of the brain harmonizing, heightening, the healing. Now the hands are moved on top of the crown. The soul star is in the heart, pulsating, filling the heart with the energy of love. It overflows into the arms and hands and radiates out from the palms into the crown, to the brain, right through the center of the body all the way to the root.

Keep your tongue touching the roof of your mouth, bring your hands over the brow, with the right palm over the brow area, the left hand on top of the right hand. Touch gently without pressure. Now visualize your soul star in the heart pulsating the energy of unconditional love. It overflows into the hands and pulsates into the third eye, which corresponds to the pituitary gland and the hypothalamus. The energy heightens, harmonizes, creates a sense of wholeness and health. Now slowly bring the hands over the nose, lips and chin, then to the throat, where they come to rest. The star is in the heart, it pulsates the energy of unconditional love. The energy overflows into the shoulders, down the arms into the hands which radiate the energy into the throat harmonizing, heightening, balancing and nurturing. Now the hands move just below the throat over the upper portion of the sternum or breast bone, corresponding to the thymus gland. The star is in the heart; it pulsates the energy of love that overflows into the arms, hands and radiates from the palms into the center of the upper chest to all those vital structures heightening, harmonizing, nurturing and healing.

Now move the hands over the heart. The heart is filled with the energy of love that pulsates from the soul star. It overflows into the shoulders, down the arms, into the hands, and the palms radiate it back into the heart so that a circuit is formed. Since the movement of the energy is in the circle, an energy now pulsates into the heart, into the circulatory system to all parts of the body, healing, harmonizing and nurturing. Now move the hands over the solar plexus, the solar plexus immediately senses the flow of energy. Then receive the soul star in the heart, pulsating, filling, overflowing into our hands which radiate the energy of love into the solar plexus heightening, harmonizing, healing. Release all negative emotions. Strengthen yourself against the emotional impact of the outside world. Now move your hands over the navel area. (Men do thrity-six clockwise rotations or spirals followed by twenty-four counterclockwise. Women do the opposite, thrity-six counterclockwise, twenty-four clockwise.

Pause

Now take the star to the upper pubic area, the sexual energy zone and then to the root. Allow it to spiral up to the center of the body, forming a channel of white light through the top of the head, the crown, on up to the transpersonal zone. The star moves down again; your arms should be up and extended. The star touches the right palm and the right foot and the left foot and the left hand and then the crown, the right elbow, the right knee, left knee, left elbow, the brow of the third eye, then down to the root, the base of the spine, then up to the throat where spirals down to the sexual zone, then up to the mid-chest, and into the solar plexus, into the spleen, and into the heart. "I am the soul. I am the light divine. I am love. I am will. I am fixed design. Go forth now and love."

"This exercise initially seems complex and difficult, but after practicing it a few times, it begins to flow easily. The rewards for your effort will be great, as this exercise will balance the energy centers of the body which correspond to the endocrine organs and nerve plexuses of the nervous system. An indescribable sense of well being will ensue." — *Joseph G. Spano, M.D.*

Grief

62

Grieving

Guide: Jule Scotti Post, M.S.

The Journey

With our breath, we take in life, energy and love. As we breathe out we let go, we release, we empty ourselves to allow the new life to flow into us. Breathe out deeply, from the lower part of your lungs, from your belly, from your deep center, empty yourself. And now slowly let the air flow in, the life force, filling you, your chest expanding gently as your lungs are slowly filled to capacity.

The out flowing and in flowing of our breath. The ebb and flow of the tides. The exchange of energy between the earth and the heavens. We live and move and have our being between the breathing in and breathing out of life.

Now in your mind's eye, see yourself in the woods on a beautiful day, late in the summer. See the trees covered in green, hear the birds singing and smell the fragrance of wild flowers. You have been filled by the rich harvest of summer fruit; the earth has given you renewed strength and support to nurture you on your journey. And now invite those you love to join you in the woods, surrounding you, holding you. You feel strong arms around you and you feel your feet firmly on the earth. Pause to take in the depth of love calling to you.

Pause

Now allow the passing of time, the days, the weeks, the months as Earth moves from season to season. You feel a coolness in the breeze as it blows through the trees. The sun's light is gentler now, and the leaves are changing color — red, gold, orange, although some are still green. Smell the dampness of the fall. Hear the quiet forest. Now the birds have flown. Now your loved ones have gone away, and you are walking through the woods alone, feeling the loss of love, of days gone by, longing for what you had, longing more for what you never had. Be aware of whatever you need to grieve.

Pause

Now as you breathe out, allow the deep sadness in your heart to flow up and fill you. Be aware of this feeling in your body. Perhaps a tightness, a heaving in your chest, perhaps a burning in your throat, a wetness in your eyes, an aching in your head. Feel the deep pain in your heart. Breathe deeply into your heart. Breathe it out. Let it go, get it flowing, get it up to your eyes, let it pour in waves of tears or long deep sobbing — let your grief, your longing, your loss, your yearning, your cry from the depth express itself in its own way according to your own deep, inner wisdom. Continue to breathe in and breathe out.

Pause

See how the trees become more and more beautiful as their colors change, and they prepare to release their summer green for the stillness of winter. You also become more beautiful as you grieve, as you change, as you let go and become still. Go deep into your stillness for the seeds of new life are there awaiting you. Breathe in and breathe out, feel the inspiration that comes with letting go.

Look how the leaves fall from the trees. The branches let them go. The branches bare themselves to the cold wind. The leaves pile up to crunch under your feet. You can also let go of whatever needs to die in you to make way for new life.

Feel in your heart the new possibilities for life as you allow the old, the past, the gone, to leave, to die.

Feel within yourself the perfect balance of life coming into you and flowing out of you. Let your breath flow gently, peacefully, in rhythm and harmony.

Now gradually begin to bring yourself back, leaving behind whatever you are releasing. Bring back with you peaceful-ness, acceptance and relaxation. Gradually allow your eyes to open, see the room around you, hear any sounds in the room. Take a few moments to become fully awake and alert. Breathe. Breathe.

"I use this imagery to help work through the grief of loss, through death, divorce, loss of a job, a home, a vision, a dream. We also need to grieve the lack of those things we never had, our childhood needs that were never met, our longings for love, for peace, for joy that have never been fulfilled." — *Jule Scotti Post, M.S.*

63

Sailing Through Grief

Guide: Christopher S. Rubel, Rel. D.

The Journey

Allow yourself to breathe deeply and feel comfortable, putting aside the felt-demands of calls unreturned, paperwork not finished, and anything that might distract you. Find yourself at the helm of a sailboat. It is a beautiful afternoon. The sea is quite calm. There is just enough helm to be comfortable, and your sloop seemingly is steering herself on an easy course.

You are alone. The boat is moving easily. There's no need to touch the lines, as long as your wind remains westerly. You see dolphins off the port stern. They are gliding gently about the same speed as your boat. You are more peaceful than you've been in months and have a sense of what it means to "follow your bliss." A small flying fish emerges and skims the surface for a distance, and as it re-enters the water with a small splash, you become more relaxed and your breathing is deeper, all the way to the bottom of your lungs, breathing slowly, deeply. Your mind is cleared of everything back at the mainland. You have been quiet for several hours, not even hearing your own voice, not whistling, not singing, just listening to the rigging and the water spinning off the bow and the stern, mixing in with your wake.

Suddenly, appearing with no warning, a tiny, yellow, warbler, with a black crown around his head, alights on one of the lines, just about a foot from your right hand. You say, "Hello," and watch him. He cocks his head this way and that, seeming to study you. He is about as big as a tennis ball and appears to be breathing very hard. He says, "Hello." You're startled, but intrigued. He continues, "My name is Warren." You tell him your name. You sail for a few minutes. Then you ask him, "Warren, where did you come from?" He answers, "I have been flying for days, tossed around higher than I've ever been, nearly frozen, and I'm completely lost. I thought I was going to land in the ocean and drown. I found this boat just in time." He is out of breath and takes a few minutes to continue. You listen to his small voice carefully, amazed at how clearly he speaks.

He says, "There were many others, and I don't know what happened to them. We were all together when the storm took us up and tossed us for hours. I think I was even unconscious through my trip," he says. You empathize with him saying, "It must be frightening to experience what you have been through." Then, you say, "I'm glad you landed on my little sloop and are safe, now." He says, "I feel so relieved and safe being aboard your boat. I was so far from home." He becomes very quiet. His tiny, feathered body is balanced on the line as the boat gently moves this way and that beneath his feet. You think of times you have felt far from home. You tell Warren you are glad he is with you and is speaking to you on this beautiful day in the channel. "Thank you for coming," you say.

You watch Warren and lazily tend your boat. Warren is hungry, and you don't know what to do. He obviously hasn't rested, eaten, or had anything to drink for too long. He's been a victim of weather and turbulence. He is certainly an alien. You find some ways you are alike. About this time, there is a woman appearing, coming up the stairs into the cockpit from the cabin and she has some cereal and some water in small bowls. She places them next to the rail on the cabin top and Warren quickly hops over to have breakfast. You watch the two of them. She is just a few inches from him as he eats and watches her. Her face is radiant and placid, bewitching to you. There was no effort in her appearing topside, and the gifts for Warren seemed to have been part of her fingertips.

"Who are you?" you ask. She looks directly at you, with a soft, somehow wry smile. She says, "You wouldn't know. You've never taken the time it would take to know me." She turns back to Warren, and you watch the two of them, again, feeling tremendous curiosity. You think to yourself, 'Who is this woman and how would I have known her?'

Pause

Again, you ask, "Who are you?" She again looks at you. Her look is one of almost teasing scorn. You come to realize she is challenging you to go inside yourself and find who she is. She has some kind of long-term agenda with you. She says, "It won't be easy for you, but you might get to know me, if you are willing to gradually give up your attachments and limitations and follow me. I am all you have ever lost and all you have always longed for. I am all you have rejected and all you have refused to feel. I am all you have been unable to love and all of those who have loved you and not been able to reach you. You will not know me, now, easily. But, you may, if you simply ask to do so and will follow me."

You are curious. You know the feelings may seem to sweep you away, but you are not afraid of her now. As you concentrate on these feelings, you know you are being led to an important, perhaps spiritual place by her. There is something haunting and profound about her. You begin to follow her, leaving the boat and entering the water. Although you slide beneath the surface, you are able to breathe. She moves gracefully ahead of you, leading you on in an unknown direction. Swimming as fast as you can you cannot keep up with her, and you lose her, completely in the blur of the water and kelp ahead of you and around you. You come to the surface and see your sailboat, sailing by itself and swim as hard as you can, but you can not catch up to the boat. You wonder if you can keep going, and your life seems suddenly in the balance, but more precious than ever. You know this is the end of your life as you have been living it. Everything you have left behind is in shreds, undone, incomplete, and nothing is prepared for your possible drowning. You swim as hard as you can, hoping for some chance to get back on board, feeling just a bit of a fool and as though you have been tricked by a fantasy. You are deeply challenged and swim with everything you have, somehow less desperate, somehow more excited. You feel your life is more important to you than it has ever seemed.

It is clear to you now, that all your priorities have been upside down. Your unlived life is very evident to you. You are aware of deeper feelings and an openness to yourself you have not had before, or at least, for a long time. In the water, ahead, you see the form of the spirit woman, swimming. In a muffled, haunting tone, her voice reaches out to you, through the water, "I love you. Do you hear me? I love you. You are just fine. Keep on swimming and listen to me. I love you."

You ask her, "Where are you?" She answers, "It doesn't matter. Just swim." You feel somehow lifted in the water, and there is a new strength coming to you, as you press on toward the boat, sailing on her own, not too far off. You draw closer to the boat and see a small, yellow ball of bird, riding on the cabin top. In the cockpit, there are several people, watching you. You draw closer. They seem glad to see you. The stern ladder is down and you grab hold of it and pull yourself up. In the cockpit are several people, who, at first, are not familiar to you. You look at them, letting your feelings come to focus and you realize you have not seen these people for a long, long time. You begin to recognize the faces and, as you do, you are able to feel a connection with each person in that sailboat cockpit.

Very slowly, now, one at a time, there are smiles of recognition. As you climb out of the water to the deck of the boat and step over the railing and into the cockpit of the sloop, one at time, the people there put arms around you. You feel the healing warmth of their arms. You are able to tell each person something you have needed to say. Then, you listen, and hear what each person has to say to you.

Pause

Look inside, at this moment, and detect elements of yourself coming together into new patterns. There is a growing sense of healing and restoration rising within you. Perhaps the people in that cockpit with you change, and you are able to be reunited, reconciled with others in your life at this moment. It is a mystical, spiritual, healing time for you. You realize it is for the others too. Let yourself stay in this setting for as long as you like.

Pause

Close ahead, off the bow, is a special island. It is a very peaceful place ,and you are gliding in very calm waters toward that mooring at this moment. With the sails down and stowed, the boot glides effortlessly toward her mooring. Again, the inner voice comes, softly and confidently calling your name, several times, arousing your attention. The voice says, "I give you that peace which passes all human understanding." The voice becomes the voice of someone you love, perhaps someone you have missed or from whom you have felt estranged. The voice may change as it speaks, but you will recognize the speaker as the words become clear to you.

It is also clear the task is to return to this place often, to let these feelings of healing deepen. Your project in "walking the mystical path with practical feet" is to return to this place as often as you like, letting go of felt-demands, relaxing, taking the deep breaths, and letting go, returning to this sailboat, this mooring. As you breath deeply and return slowly to a more alert, invigorated present place, feeling confident, feeling the strength returning to your body, there is another word from deep within you. You recognize the voice of the woman on the boat, as she says to you, "You are a child of the universe. You have a right to be centered, peaceful, healed, and free of all grief and pain. You have a gift of receiving this healing and living fully in the present, with more to give than ever before."

Enough! Let it deepen. Cherish this awareness. Let your heart receive this. Let consciousness absorb this healing, revitalizing journey. Each time you repeat this journey, you will be strengthened and enriched by the images, the feelings, the words, as you realize increasing peace of mind, courage, and desire to give and receive in closer relationships.

"The guided imagery, Sailing Through Grief, was initially a process I used myself to assist in getting through some long endured feelings of grief and unfinished business with important people in my life. I found, in following these images, a well of emotions became available to me. Upon completion, each time, I experienced a sense of healing and exhilaration. It was clear to me, this journey was helpful and I have since utilized this with several clients. Each time, the person has been able to release emotions long repressed and feel more available for relationships, more lively, and less compulsive. It is clearer to me now how repressed grief functions to keep us "stuck" in addictive behaviors and tendencies towards isolation. Have a good sail and keep tacking towards consciousness." — Christopher S. Rubel, Rel. D.

Past Lives

64

Past Life Regression

Guide: Chrystle Clae

The Journey

Take a seated, comfortable position, free of any distur-
bances. Begin to breathe deeply. In through your nose, hold
to a mental count of five. Exhale slowly, through slightly
parted lips. Repeat this process one more time. Continuing
to breathe deeply, do some slow, very gentle neck rolls. Let
your chin slowly fall to your chest until you feel the tension
in the back of your neck. Take a deep breath into the tension
and feel it relax and release. Bring your neck back up to
center and let your right ear gently fall towards your right
shoulder. Don't raise your shoulder to meet your ear. Just let
it fall, until you feel the tension in the left side of your neck.
Again, breathe into this tension and release it. Relax it. Now,
let your head slowly drop backward so that your chin seems
to reach for the ceiling. You feel a slight tension in the front
of your throat. Again, breathe into this tension; relax it,
release it. Bring your head back to center and let your left ear
fall gently and slowly towards your left shoulder until you
feel the tension in the right side of your neck. Once more,
you breathe very deeply into this tension and feel it instantly

relax and release. Another deep breath, in through the nose and out, slowly, through slightly parted lips. Once more, and this time imagine that, as you inhale, the breath you inhale slowly is a soft, blue, powdery vibration that fills your lungs and your body with a feeling of the soft blue. Hold to another count of five. Exhale slowly and gently, through slightly parted lips, a soft pink vibration. A loving vibration that completely encircles you within and without.

Now, sitting back with your palms up, feel the energy of the earth under your feet. It's warm and comforting. Let your feet feel like they almost melt into the earth. Feel very grounded, stable and certain of where you are. Tighten the feeling in the muscles in your feet. As you exhale, release those muscles and feel them soothed and free of tension. Now, tighten the muscles in your calf. Release it. Tighten the muscles in your thighs and buttocks. Now, release. Tighten the muscles in your stomach. Take a deep breath and release those muscles, relax them. You've massaged them and warmed them. Feel the muscles in your chest and your shoulders tighten. As you breathe deeply, you release and relax all the tensions and tightness you've been holding in your shoulders and chest. Now, make a fist with each hand and tighten it. Take a deep breath. As you exhale, release those fists and feel the tingly vibrations in your fingers which are relaxed and warm. Tighten the muscles in your face, around your eyes and jaw. Make them real tight. Take a deep breath and relax and release all those tensions that you've been holding in those muscles. Tighten the skull, the top of your head. With one more deep, deep breath, as you exhale, release your whole skull and top of your head. Feel your whole body completely comfortable and relaxed — relaxed, but feeling heavy, almost like there's a lead weight that is holding you still.

Continuing to breath deeply, imagine that you are in a hall, a long hall. At the end of this hall, you can see that there is an elevator. Walk slowly towards this elevator. Realize that you are alone but feel very comfortable. As you approach the elevator, it opens. As the doors open, you enter this elevator. Once inside you see that it's brightly lit with color that's very comfortable for you. In this elevator there's a cozy chair for you to sit in. The doors close and you look above them to see, by the number that's lit, that you're on the eighth floor. As the eighth floor light goes off, the elevator begins to descend.

The lighting around you changes to a beautiful, soft lavender. Continue to watch the numbers above the door, as the number seven lights. Again, as the light goes off, know that it begins to descend and the light around you becomes blue. Sense how you feel as the lighting changes. Above the door you notice the number six light up. Again, the number goes off and you begin to descend once more. The lighting around you changes to a blue, a vibrant blue color. Once more, the number light shows and it's the number five. Continuing to breath deeply you notice that the light goes out and, again, you begin to descend. This time the lighting changes to a soft yellow, and you realize the difference in how you feel in this yellow light vibration. You become more and more relaxed as you notice the number four light up above the door. You know as it goes out that you're descending once more. The lighting changes to an orange, a vibrant orange. An orange that gives you a sense of courage and ambition, anticipation for your journey. The number three lights up above the door. Again, the light goes off when you descend, lower and lower and more and more relaxed. The lighting around you becomes red. Now, above the door, you see the number two. Breathe deeply, more and more relaxed. The light goes out on the number, and the lighting around you gives up a beautiful, golden feel. All around you is gold. Realize how you feel with gold vibrations. As you descend, lower and lower and more and more relaxed, the light above the door shows you number one. As the car settles, the doors open.

Still breathing deeply, you look out from these open doors to a cold and dark room. Feel the emptiness in this room. Continuing to breathe deeply, feeling safe and relaxed, you now hold a candle. The candle is magically, instantly lit so that you can see further ahead in this room. It has a lower, sunken section. It's up ahead. It's where you're beginning to see a glimmer of light as you walk closer and closer. You see steps leading down to a warm and bright sunken fireplace. Blow out your candle. The light from the fireplace is fine. Slowly, walk on these worn stone stairs leading down to the fireplace. On the first step going down, you feel the warmth and the glow from the fireplace on your feet and ankles. Going down the second step, the warmth is felt in your calves and knees. Going down still, to the third, your thighs feel warm. Going down to the fourth, the trunk of your body, your stomach and your back are warm in the glow of this wonderful fireplace. As you go down to the fifth step, your shoulders are warmed. Down the final stair, the sixth step, your neck and your face, your whole body is basking in the glow of this warm, relaxing, crackling fireplace.

Listen to it crackling. Now, see that there is a beautiful, golden, circular ledge around this fireplace. Continuing to breathe deeply, you're comforted by this fire. You notice a soft cushion in your favorite color is waiting for you. As you sit, you gaze comfortably at the jumping, beautiful flames in front of you. You feel released from your shell of a body and understand the energy that is you, as you say to yourself "I am me. I am me. I am me." You gaze at the fire and a radiant light-being emerges from the fire to sit beside you.

You're thrilled as you see this light-being. You feel completely safe and at ease. This being telepathically tells you that it's your guide, your guide to your past. This being of light takes your hand and immediately you feel a sense of peace and light, of unconditional love. This being loves you just as you are. Truly you're protected, and you know it won't harm you in any way. Together you walk into the flame completely protected, completely immersed in cool, brilliant light. You are confident, safe and free. Your light guide tells you that you're approaching a period of time when you lived many, many years ago in another lifetime, a past life. Continuing to breathe deeply, very comfortable and completely relaxed, you sense that, with your guide beside you, you'll experience no anxiety or pain. No negative results that may have happened in this past lifetime will affect you now. You're simply an observer. And, remember, you're not alone. Your guide touches your third eye area, the area between your eyebrows. You suddenly feel a surge of energy. This surge of energy sends your mind whirling. You're whirling and whirling. When the touch is removed you feel very grounded and realize you've traveled through time.

Instinctively, you look down at your feet. What do you see? What type of shoes? What size feet? Are you surprised? Can you tell what sex you are from your feet? Now, look at the road that you're standing on. Is this road well traveled or is it hardly used? You now realize that you are walking into your home; the place that you live... the place that you lived in this past life. Look at the countryside around you. Do you recognize it as a place that you identify? How does it feel?

What type of climate do you sense around you? Breathe it in. Now, you see the place that you live in just ahead, off to your left. You know what country you're in. It's your country. Now, with another deep breath, quickly go to the door of your home and open it. Is anyone there to greet you? If there is, sense now what relationship they have to you. How are they dressed? Is there anything special that you feel from these people? If there's one special person there, look into his or her eyes. Know now if this person has come into your present life in another form. What relationship do you have with this person in your present life? Why have you come together? To work out a lesson that needs to be learned? To finish a goal together? Know, as you look into his or her eyes, why you may have come together again. Now, look around the dwelling. Notice anything on the walls? Any decorations, anything that comes to your awareness? Look at the floor. What is that like? Is there any distinctive smell in this place? What kind of lighting is there?

Pause

The evening meal is being prepared, and you've been told to come sit down. You go to eat it. If there are others there, they join you. If you're sitting at a table what position do you take? Can you tell how old you are? Now, look around the table, and if there are others, view these others with the understanding of why you are together. Take your time.

Pause

Look at your meal. What is this that's before you to eat? Who prepared this meal? Was it prepared in love? Is there anyone at this dinner scene that you sense has come again with you in your present life experience? Look into their eyes. Understand why you were together in this past life experience and why you've come together in your present life.

Pause

Now, get a strong feeling, a sense of the most important lesson you had to learn in this lifetime of long ago. What was your purpose or goal for this lifetime? Is it a lesson that you completed, or is it one that you've brought with you in this lifetime? Instantly feel these answers.

Pause

Is there anything in this past time that would relieve you or help you understand a problem in this current lifetime? Realize this now.

Pause

Continuing to relax, and breathing deeply, you're comfortable and at ease and so thankful for this information. Your light guide once again appears to you, right beside you, and again, touches that special spot between your eyebrows. You once again whirl. Your mind whirls and whirls until you find yourself in another lifetime, a lifetime where you were filled with love. In this lifetime you knew you were joined with your soul mate. Look, as this person approaches. Notice the outstretched arms, the total feeling of love and acceptance. Look into these loving eyes and feel the completeness. The feeling of being loved just as you are. Just for the you that's inside. Let this beloved one embrace you. Feel your unity, your oneness — the overwhelming sense of love. Now, looking once more into this person's eyes, do you recognize this person in your present life? It may be a totally different relationship, but you'll get the same feel from these eyes.

Pause

If you've come together again in this current lifetime, know now what you need to accomplish with this person. Don't think about it, just observe your first impression.

Pause

As I count backwards from five to one, your guide removes it's touch. Five, four, three, two, one. You're once more alone, walking back to your comfortable spot in your current home. Again, as I count backwards from five to one, slowly awaken, remembering everything you've experienced today. Five, breathing deeply. Four, slowly awakening refreshed. Three, beginning to wiggle your toes. Two, wiggling your fingers. One, feeling completely refreshed, slowly open your eyes at a pace that's comfortable for you. Be filled with love and light and peace.

Now is the time to write down any experiences. Any insight or understandings into current relationships or current life purpose. From this day on, your life is enriched, beautifully enhanced with the feeling of unconditional love. A feeling that vibrates to all living things from the you, the inner you, with no judgement, no pain, nothing but love, light and peace to go forward with your life's work. May you have a life filled with light, peace and unconditional love.

"Whether you remember a valid former lifetime or simply make up a story from your subconscious - you will understand the 'reason' for current relationships, talents, difficulties and choices."
— *Chrystle Clae*

Male/Female

65

Aphrodite

Guide: Mary Ellen Carne, Ph.D.

The Journey

Go to that quiet place, your center; focus on your breathing to get there. Let go, and when you are ready, feel yourself descending a spiral staircase that brings you to the place within, where you find your power. The best way to know the Goddess Aphrodite is to experience her within yourself.

Pause

Descend your spiral stairs and when you reach the bottom, find yourself on a beach, a warm, beautiful sunlit beach. Allow your eyes to look around and take in all that is there for you.... Now find your eyes looking out over the water, a beautiful, sparkly, clear, blue-green, ocean — a fathomless, ever-shifting sea, symbol of the essential female. Allow yourself to really "be" in this place of yours; take in its sights, sounds, smells and sensations. Take a moment to explore this special place of yours.

It is here in this splendid place that you will encounter Aphrodite. Aphrodite — golden one, primal mother of all creation, woman born of the foam of the sea…. Aphrodite — mediator between earth, sky and sea, our inner goddess who outwardly manifests herself to us as morning dew, the mist, or cloud, as fertilizing rain and as the sea.

Out on your ocean now, see Aphrodite carried along on the waves in the soft foam of the sea, accompanied by her sea nymph companions…. This is Aphrodite, virgin goddess in the original sense, one in herself, sensual but always independent, a blend of receptivity and focus. She is the intense love and understanding that connects, creates and begets all life. Have her move closer now. Aphrodite, a friendly, smiling, laughter-loving goddess who combines wild animal desire with the sophisticated arts of love. Her intelligence is intuitive, she harbors no anxieties or ambivalence about sex and her body, for she knows that she alone owns her body….

Let her now approach you and have her place a sparkling golden shawl around your shoulders and say to you, "Remember always that this goldenness of womanhood is eternally yours. You are Aphrodite, a part of me." You dance for a moment on that sunlit beach, celebrating this golden being that is woman, that is you.

Pause

Once you have finished, Aphrodite approaches you once again and hands you a beautiful shell that she has brought with her from the sea. She lovingly gives it to you saying, "I give this as a symbol of your sexuality, that which belongs to no one but yourself. Rejoice in your power. No one but you may own or control your body. All acts of love of your choosing are my rituals. Let there be beauty and strength in your body, power and compassion, honor and humility, mirth and reverence felt in every cell of your being. Experience your sexuality as a force of transformation, not of possession or being possessed. Tap the Aphrodite energy that urges you to dance radiantly, to flow, soar and glow in joyful appreciation of your whole being...."

You are fully with Aphrodite now, alchemical goddess, the golden one, soul of the world, energy whose presence gives luster and brightness. Her energy shines forth from within, which like a magnet, draws waves of loving energy to you.... Aphrodite's love is a love far greater than just romantic or sexual love. She is also platonic love, self-love, deep friendship, soul connection, rapport and empathetic understanding. All are expressions of the love that Aphrodite draws to herself.

Pause

And now it is time to view the ever-present "other side" of this wondrous alchemical force that is Aphrodite, for along with the strength of love comes strong passions of hate, rivalry, and jealousy as well.... Emotions that can provoke others to murder, to go to war, to feud with friends and relatives — Aphrodite's dark side. The love Aphrodite can arouse may sometimes turn to hate just as the consequences of love can sometimes be disastrous. Aphrodite's urge toward sweet desire, intense yearning, regardless of the end toward which it is directed, can lead to great suffering as well as joy, making her presence a sometimes frightening experience. While Aphrodite's energy is indispensable to life and creativity, if left uncontrolled, her power can also be all-consuming and destructive to our "selves." Yet Aphrodite *never* lets you forget that you *always* have choice and control in keeping a rein on her emotions.

Pause

Lead yourself back now to your sunlit beach, rejoicing in your experience of *all* of Aphrodite. Sensing your wholeness, feel once again the warmth of the sun's rays, the ocean spray and the day's golden glow.... On your beach, in preparation for leaving her presence, create a sacred space in Aphrodite's honor, a place resplendent with symbols of her presence, the dolphin, the dove, the swan and sparrow, a golden apple, pearls from the sea, a beautiful shell, a lily, watermine, a rose or any other symbol that arises for you from your own inner place of Aphrodite.... Create a space of honor for her within you, a place to which you may return whenever you so choose.

Pause

Aphrodite, the golden one, is the power, glory and magnetism of all forms of love. She embodies the aspect of the *feminine that of her own choosing* seeks relationship and union with "others." Find a way now to leave your beach and gradually return to the present bringing with you the memory of Aphrodite, flower goddess, she who whispers from the ocean, lover of laughter, giver of joy. Where she walks, the earth blooms beneath her feet and draws forth the hidden promise of life. Remember, she is always and forever a part of you.

"I use this guided imagery in a class entitled Wisdom Within - Self Discovery through Myth, Symbol and Imagery. It helps people to experience and claim the archetypal energy of Aphrodite."
— *Mary Ellen Carne, Ph.D.*

66

Male Development

Guide: Loyd White, Ph.D.

The Journey

Close your eyes or see a focal point on the ceiling. Take three deep cleansing breaths and relax.

Pause

Get comfortable with both feet on the floor. Experience Mother Earth's energies coming up through your feet. Feel her energies coursing up through your legs and all the way to your heart — the center of your compassion. Extend your right hand and allow Father Sky to touch your fingers. Take the energy of Father Sky in your hand as if it is a ball of white energy. Now take the energy of Father Sky and gradually move this energy toward your heart. Take this ball of energy and place it in your heart. Experience the uniting of Mother Earth and Father Sky. In this uniting, you experience the coming together of all your ancestors.

Pause

Now I'm going to count down from ten to zero and as I do you will become even more deeply relaxed. ten... relaxing nine... relaxing even more eight... seven... six... relaxing five... four... three... deeper and deeper relaxed two... and one... and all the way relaxed. As you reach zero, going all the way down, you see a door marked "The Pass." You pass through the door and enter all the way into your imagination. You are on a journey.

In your journey you come to a meadow by a mountain... you take whatever equipment you need for your ascent up the mountain... prior to your ascent, you take a vessel out of your backpack and view it in detail.

Pause

You begin your climb. At first it is a rather easy climb. Midway you stop for a rest and observe how far you have come.

Pause

You continue your ascent until you reach a precipice where you are stuck... you can neither go up nor down... a wise man extends his hand down and assists you to the summit... standing on the summit you observe the world below and then allow the sun to penetrate you... the sun's rays pull you into its center.

Pause

You come back down to the mountain top and observe the earth below... you descend to the meadow by the mountain.

You take the vessel out again and observe it inside and out for any changes.

Pause

Now, leave this journey behind you and begin to come back to this reality. As you do take this experience with you.

One... coming up, two... even further, three... by the time you reach the top you will feel wonderfully good in every way, four... and five... begin to be aware of your surroundings, six... your senses become alive and you hear the sounds around you, seven... feeling very peaceful and calm — yet very alert, we reach eight... and you take three deep easy cleansing breaths, nine... and ten... that brings you all the way back to the surface feeling peaceful, calm, yet very alert.

"The vessel filled with spirit is symbolic of the transformation process Jung named individuation. In this particular guided imagery four phases of male development are identified: 1. Son's focus on mother 2. Son's movement toward and obedience to father 3. Challenge of father and son's movement toward self will and self determination 4. The son's spiritual integration with father. In the primitive cultures, the son was called out. Through guided imagery, modern man is able to activate his inner symbolic nature thereby reclaiming the father image as in the Native American Pueblo Tale, 'Arrow to the Sun'."

— Loyd White, Ph.D.

Appendix

Sharing Your Journey

Because the creative mind is a gift that all human beings should cherish and expand, the editors of this volume are eager to learn about your visualizations and imageries.

This is the first of ten volumes. If you use guided imagery and are interested in sharing your journeys, we would like to hear from you. For consideration in our next volume, please send submissions to or contact:

United States Publishing
3485 Mercantile Avenue
Naples, Florida 33942
(813) 643-7787
Fax (813) 643-3989
Attn: "Guided Imagery Volume Two"
New Journeys

Contacting the Guides

If you would like to contact any of the guides whose journeys appeared in this volume, please send your request to:

United States Publishing
3485 Mercantile Avenue
Naples, Florida 33942
Attn: "Guided Imagery Volume One"
(Please include Guides Names)